WONDERS
OF THE WORLD

SANDRA FORTY

Published by TAJ Books 2007

27, Ferndown Gardens,
Cobham,
Surrey,
UK,
KT11 2BH

www.tajbooks.com

All notations of errors or omissions (author inquiries, permissions) concerning the content of this book
should be addressed to TAJ Books 27, Ferndown Gardens, Cobham, Surrey, UK, KT11 2BH, info@tajbooks.com.

ISBN: 978-1-84406-091-7

Printed in China.
1 2 3 4 5 10 09 08 07

INTRODUCTION

▲

The Pyramids at Giza, Egypt

If time and money were no object, where would you go and what would you see? This planet is such an amazing place that there is something of astounding interest in every part of the world. So, to make the decision easier we present here in no particular order other than geographical, a compilation of the most interesting and spectacular places to see—a combination of natural wonders and man-made structures from all around the world. Most of these places, of course, are major tourist attractions, and many of us have at least one of them within easy traveling distance—we should all attempt to see at least one of them for the sheer scale and ambition of these places is way beyond everyday experience.

It was during the second century B.C. in Ancient Greece that the first listing of the wonders of the world was drawn up. The list, naturally, was limited to their known world—essentially the lands around Greece and the Mediterranean. Many of the wonders we identify today—especially the natural ones, but also those in the kingdom of China such as the astonishing Great Wall—were unknown to them and so are obvious omissions from the list. This earliest known selection is credited to Antipater of Sidon who named seven ancient structures, but no natural features. However, it wasn't until the Middle Ages that the definitive list of the Seven Wonders of the World was finalized, by which time already most of the wonders had ceased to exist. They are in chronological order:

The **Great Pyramid of Giza**, was built by the Pharaoh Khufu (also known by the Greek version of his name, Cheops) in 2,550 B.C. to house his remains when he died. It has long been the only remaining one of the seven wonders to survive the test of time, a fact that is more remarkable as it is also the most ancient. It was built over about 20 years in the necropolis town of Giza, itself part of ancient Memphis, now on the outskirts of Cairo in Egypt. When it was finished the Great Pyramid peaked at 481ft (146m) high and was the tallest man-made object on the planet for over 43 centuries. It contains approximately two million blocks of stone, each of which weighs over two tons. It is still a mystery how such a monumental structure was built. Over the years the pyramid has lost some 30ft (10m) from its top and its original covering of smooth casing stones. It is orientated exactly to face due north, south, east, and west, at an angle of slope of 51 degrees and 51 minutes. The other two pyramids at Giza are not included as part of the wonders of the world.

The **Hanging Gardens of Babylon**, were probably built by King Nebuchadnezzar II (604–562 B.C.) to please his wife who longed for her greener homeland, but their existence and even location have never been established, although they were probably somewhere on the east bank of the great Euphrates river. The only descriptions of the gardens come from much later Ancient Greek sources and may possibly be an exaggerated conglomeration of accounts of lush plantings in an arid land—so it is possible that this wonder never existed except in legend.

The Athenian sculptor Pheidia was commissioned in 435 B.C. to create the **Statue of Zeus at Olympia** from to stand in the god's magnificent temple. The statue was made of gold and ivory and showed the god seated with the top of his crown virtually touching the ceiling. The statue was 40ft high (13m), and had Zeus stood up he would have shattered the temple, a fact that intrigued and awed spectators. The statue attracted worshippers from around Greece and was so magnificent that the Emperor Caligula even attempted to take it back to Rome. After surviving floods and earthquakes some wealthy Greeks transported the statue to a palace in Constantinople where it was eventually destroyed by fire in 462 A.D.

The fourth wonder is the great marble **Temple of Artemis at Ephesus** (now in Turkey) which was built by the Greeks in 550 B.C. Built for the goddess of hunting, wild nature, and fertility, this was considered to be the most beautiful building in the world. It was commissioned by King Croesus and designed by the Greek architect Chersiphron. After serving as a temple and thriving market place, it was burned down on the night of July 21, 356 B.C. by a man named Herostratus who did so solely to immortalize himself. Legend has it that Artemis was distracted at the time in Macedonia overseeing the birth of the baby who would grow up to be Alexander the Great. Artemis was said to be too preoccupied to save her magnificent temple, the destruction of which was later taken to be an auspicious omen for Alexander.

The vast **Mausoleum of Maussollos at Halicarnassus** (now Bodrum in southwest Turkey) was built in 351 B.C. Nothing is known about king Maussollos himself except that he was deemed worthy of such a monument—apparently the idea of his wife and sister Artemisia. It was completed three years after his death and remained sound for 16 centuries until an earthquake caused damage to the colonnade and roof. Then the Knights of St. John of Malta conquered the area in the early 15th century and built a vast castle nearby. When this was fortified in 1494 they cannibalized the Mausoleum for stone and by 1522 it had disappeared into the fabric of the castle.

The **Colossus of Rhodes** was a giant statue of the sun god Helios that in popular mythology straddled the harbor entrance of this eastern Mediterranean island. In fact archaeologists have calculated that this position would have been impossible and a more likely site for the statue was on a nearby promontory. It was built in 292 B.C. to celebrate the unity of the island's three kingdoms and of their peace treaties with Egypt and Macedonia. The statue was designed by local sculptor Chares of Lindos and took 12 years to complete. Helios stood on a white marble plinth and was built from the feet up with an iron and stone framework covered with bronze skin. It had a final height of about 110ft (33m) but nobody is sure of its exact stance. In about 226 B.C. a huge earthquake hit the island of Rhodes leaving many towns in ruins and fatally shaking the statue until it gave way at the knees. It had lasted for around 66 years and is the shortest-lived of the seven wonders. Ptolemy III of Egypt immediately offered to finance its restoration but a local oracle warned against the idea. Instead, it was left in ruins until the A.D. 654 Arab invasion of Rhodes when the pieces were sold to a Syrian Jew who transported them home, supposedly on the backs of 900 camels. It then disappeared into history.

For many centuries the seventh wonder was disputed: some said it should be the palace of Cyrus, king of Persia; others nominated the walls of Babylon, but by the end of the sixth century A.D. it had become accepted that the seventh wonder was the **Lighthouse at Alexandria**. This was built on the island of Pharos just outside the city of Alexandria in Egypt. The entrance to Alexandria harbor was particularly hazardous and King Ptolemy Soter conceived the idea of a lighthouse, but it was his son Ptolemy Philadelphus who completed the project. The architect was Sostratus and when it was finished it was dedicated to Ptolemy Soter and his wife Berenice. During the day the lighthouse mirror dazzled in the sunshine and at night a huge fire at its apex reflected in the mirror and warned of the surrounding dangerous waters. Fuel for the fire was pulled up the central shaft. It was said that it could be seen for miles and that the mirror could also be used to ignite and burn enemy ships. The white marble lighthouse rose in three stages up to a height of 384ft (117m). For some time after it was first built a statue of Poseidon stood at the top. Over the years the lighthouse safely guided ships around the harbor until it was badly damaged by two successive earthquakes, the first in 1303 and again in 1323. Finally, in 1480 when the port of Alexandria was fortified on the orders of Sultan Qaitbay, a fort was built on the same site using the fallen stones from the Lighthouse.

Seven Wonders of the Modern World

Since ancient times many people have compiled similar lists to comprise the modern world. The most accepted of these was drawn up by the American Society of Civil Engineers in 1994 after a worldwide poll of civil engineering societies and distinguished engineering experts. Their choices for the "Seven Wonders of the Modern World" were feats of astonishing modern engineering which had to be completed and working as well as innovative, although—unsurprisingly—weighted toward the constructs of the New World.

In chronological order they are:

The **Panama Canal** cuts miles and days off the sea voyage between east and west coasts of the Americas and is one of the greatest civil engineering feats of the early 20th century. A first attempt by the French had failed before the U.S. venture led by Colonel George Washington Goethals was successful. The work of 42,000 laborers in humid, unhygienic, dangerous, and mosquito-ridden conditions was truly heroic. Hundreds died. Eventually after blasting, dredging, and removing millions of tons of earth and rubble the canal was cut from east to west in 1914. Each ship transit loses 52 million gallons of water, but Panama has such heavy and frequent rainfall that this loss is quickly made up.

The **Empire State Building** was one of the earliest wonders of the modern world and has remained as one of the most iconic buildings of the 20th century. Work started on the site of the old Waldorf-Astoria Hotel on Fifth Avenue, New York, in March 1930 and was completed within an astonishing 14 months in May 1931. Perhaps even more astonishing is the fact that it came in under budget at $24,718,000 instead of the expected $50 million due to the catastrophic economic slump known as the Great Depression. At 102 stories it remained the tallest building in the world until 1972 and the appearance of the first of the Twin Towers of the World Trade Center.

The **Golden Gate Bridge** across the Golden Gate Strait was for many years the longest and tallest suspension bridge in the world. It is claimed that the bridge contains enough wire to encircle the world three times. It took four years to build and was completed in 1937 under budget at a cost of $35 million and ahead of schedule despite a month's setback when the Sidney M. Hauptman crashed into a construction trestle during one of San Francisco's notoriously dense fogs. Nevertheless, the Golden Gate opened to traffic at midday on May 28, 1937.

The Netherlands are not known as the Low Countries for nothing, much of their land lies below sea level and is in constant danger of being inundated with the North Sea. Consequently, the people of the Netherlands have for centuries constructed dykes and ditches, barriers and walls to keep out the waters from their lands. Land

▲
The CN Tower, or "Canada's National" Tower, in Toronto, Canada

▲

The Itaipu Dam which straddles the borders of Brazil and Paraguay

reclamation has been an ongoing Dutch project since time immemorial. One of the most ambitious projects was the **North Sea Protection Works**, the first stage of which was started in 1927. The plan was to construct a 19-mile (30.5km) long 100-yard (91m) thick enclosure dam across the neck of the Zuiderzee; this was completed in 1932 and after draining provided over half a million acres of reclaimed farmland (known as polders). Despite the "storm of the century" in 1953 the dam, although sustaining heavy damage, successfully protected the land.

The second, even more ambitious stage was the Eastern Schelde Barrier (known as the Delta Plan or Oosterschelde) across the mouth of the delta created by the rivers Rhine and Meuse in the southwest corner of the Netherlands. This surge barrier drops massive gates across 2 miles (3km) to bar the way whenever storm waters threaten to engulf the surrounding land. This was finished in 1986 although flood protection is an ongoing project for the Dutch.

The **CN Tower** in Toronto, Canada, is the world's tallest freestanding structure at 1,815ft (553m). Being so tall it had to be designed to withstand wind speeds of up to 260mph and two ten-ton counterweights are attached to the mast to diminish swaying. It took 40 months to build and went up at a rate of 18ft (5.5m) per day, opening to the public on June 26, 1976. It serves as a telecommunications center as well as a major tourist attraction.

The sixth wonder of the modern world is the **Itaipu Dam in South America**. Harnessing the power of the Parana river (Paean river) the Itaipu Dam straddles the border between Brazil and Paraguay. It is one of the largest hydroelectric power stations in the world generating 75 billion kilowatts of electricity a year, enough to provide 72 percent of Paraguay's energy needs and a good 25 percent of Brazil's. Construction on this huge project started in January 1975, finished in 1982 and cost some $20 billion to build. The dam itself is 5 miles (8km) wide and 643ft (196m) high and contains 18 massive hydroelectric generators. In the course of its construction, workers had to dig a 1.3-mile (2km) bypass and remove 50 million tons of earth and rock to divert the course of the seventh largest river in the world. To create the massive reservoir behind the dam, a huge swathe of rainforest had to be

cleared so the land could be flooded.

The final modern wonder links historic enemies England and France underground. The **Channel Tunnel** runs from Folkestone in southern England for 31 miles (50km) under the seabed to Coquelles in northern France. It is the second longest tunnel in the world and comprises three 5ft (1.5m) thick concrete tubes, of which the central tunnel is the service and emergency shaft, and the other two railroad tunnels. Also called the Euro Tunnel or Chunnel, the linking of Britain and France in such a way had been an impossible dream for many decades since Napoleon first seriously investigated the possibilities. After many years in the planning, work started in the 1970s and was completed only after massive cost overspends and delays. Work finally finished in 1993 and it opened for cross-Channel traffic the following year. It cost an estimated $12 billion to link the British Isles to Continental Europe.

Since 1994 when this list was drawn up by the American Society of Civil Engineers many even bigger civil engineering projects have been completed, it is of course an on-going process as mankind builds ever bigger and higher and more ambitiously. For example the Akashi-Kaikyo Bridge in Japan has become the longest suspension bridge in the world; Kansai International Airport, also in Japan, is built on its own entirely artificial island. In Malaysia, the astonishing Petronas Twin Towers would also make the list of modern wonders. So in the absence of an extensive and updated list we offer this book as an introduction to many of the most astounding sights to see on the planet.

Natural Wonders of the World

The world is split into five continents plus Antarctica, which was discovered as late as 1820 when it was designated the sixth continent. With the exception of the latter, there are wonders to be seen in all of them. Most early evidence of man has been discovered in Africa—Ethiopia, Kenya, Tanzania, and South Africa specifically— although in both China and Java fossil evidence has been found of early hominids. However, thousands of years had to pass before the growth of great civilizations and their grandiose building projects. It is impossible to know how many great structures were built by early man as they have long disappeared; built of transitory materials such as mud and wood, they simply crumbled back into the earth. The early civilizations that built their great buildings out of stone are the ones that have survived into recorded time. Great civilizations such as the Ancient Egyptians, the Mesopotanians, the Chinese, Cambodians, and the civilizations of Mexico and Central America have left amazing indications of the wealth and vibrancy of their cultures.

This book looks at the wonders of the world geographically and all of the areas have something to offer. Africa is the second largest continent and contains just over 20 percent of the total land area of the Earth. Roughly three-quarters of its land mass is surrounded by water: the Atlantic Ocean to the west, the Indian Ocean to the east, and the Antarctic Ocean to the south. To the north and northeast lie the land masses of Europe and Asia respectively. Africa is separated from Europe by the relatively small Mediterranean Sea and from Asia by the Isthmus of Suez across which the Suez Canal now cuts. From its most northerly point in Tunisia to the most southerly point in South Africa it is about 5,000 miles (approximately 8,000km) and almost as much east to west at its broadest point between Somalia and Cape Verde. The equator cuts across the bottom third of the continent. Fossil evidence shows that humans occupied what is now Ethiopia, Kenya. Tanzania, and South Africa up to seven million years ago. Of the great African civilizations that have come and gone over the millennia the best known is that of the Ancient Egyptians whose legacy of wonders includes the Pyramid of Giza and the magnificent temples at Abu Simbel. Three of the greatest natural wonders of the world are found in Africa. The mighty river Nile was at the heart of Ancient Egypt and their very civilization depended on the annual flood of the Nile: if the deluge did not arrive, drought and famine would follow and thousands would die. The Ancient Egyptian deity Hapy personified the flood of the Nile and it was his intervention and good will that ensured regeneration and fertility. The source of the Nile was one of the great quests for adventurers and explorers and many expeditions into the heart of Africa were made before the source—in Lake Victoria—was finally established by Lieutenant John Speke in 1858. The Nile consists of two great rivers, the White Nile that comes out of equatorial East Africa and the Blue Nile that joins the White at Khartoum in Sudan. It rises in the highlands of Ethiopia at Lake Tana following the great summer rains. The White Nile gets its name from the clay it picks up in the Sudan (where it is known as the Bahr al Jebel). The Blue Nile is so called because of its contrastingly clear waters. The two rivers converge at Khartoum where they jointly flow on into Egypt.

One of the other great wonders of continental Africa is also formed from water—the Victoria Falls that thunders between Zimbabwe and Zambia in the heart of Africa. It was first seen by western eyes in 1860 by Dr. David Livingstone. To the locals it is called Mosi-oa-Tunya, the Smoke that Thunders, and plunges with a deafening roar (especially when the river is high during the rainy season in February) in places up

▲
The mighty Victoria Falls, between Zimbabwe and Zambia, Africa

to 350ft (107m) into the Zambezi Gorge. The falls are the largest curtain of water in the world being an astonishing 5,604ft (1,708m) across.

Many things about Africa are astounding, but our third great natural wonder is the Serengeti National Park in Tanzania that provides a unique and diverse natural habitat for millions of plains animals. "Serengeti" comes from the Maasai language and means "extended place." Covering over 5,000 square miles (12,950sq km) it lies between the Great Rift Valley to the east and Lake Victoria to the west, and includes the Maasai Mara Game Reserve, the Maswa Game Reserve, and the Ngorongoro Conservation Area. The landscape itself varies between wooded grassland, open grass plains, black clay plains, volcanic plains, savannah, woodlands, and swamps. Almost 500 species of bird live here and over 30 species of large herbivores, including elephants, zebra, monkeys, and giraffe as well as large carnivores like lions, hyenas, and cheetahs.

Asia is a vast continent and the largest on the planet, although quite where it starts and Europe ends on its western frontier has changed over the centuries, usually depending on the political climate of the time. However, the general criterion is that Asia starts east of the Ural mountains and south of the Caucasus Mountains and edges around the Black Sea and Caspian Sea. The other frontiers are obvious with the great oceans providing the boundaries. Many great civilizations, religions, languages, and philosophies have come and gone in Asia; arguably, this is the area where the next great civilizations are being formed. Certainly, many of the very greatest wonders of the world are found in this region.

On Honshu island lies one of the most iconic sights for Japanese—the sacred and beautiful Mount Fuji which rises 12,388ft (3,776m) above the surrounding plain. This mountain is a dormant stratovolcano and is known to have erupted at least 16 times since 781 A.D. Two of the biggest events were in 930 B.C. and 1050 A.D. The most recent eruption was in 1707 when a vent was blown in the southeast side of the slope. Known as Fujisan to locals, on a clear day the mountain can be seen from Tokyo and Yokohama and it is a familiar image across all types of Japanese media, but especially in paintings and prints.

Asia is demarcated by huge mountain ranges that cut one country off from another, but none are bigger than the Himalayas that extend along the northern frontiers of

▲
The banks of the River Nile, Egypt

INTRODUCTION

▲

Mount Fuji, Honshu Island, Japan

Bhutan, Burma, India, Nepal, and Pakistan. They were formed millions of years ago when the Indian subcontinent drifted northwards to collide into Asia (the geological process known as plate tectonics) forcing the ground to rise. The Himalayas comprise three parallel ranges: the Greater Himalayas, the Lesser Himalayas, and the Outer Himalayas. The system runs for about 1,941 miles (2,400km) and can be up to 200 miles (330km) in width. The northern range, the Greater Himalayas, contains the three highest mountains in the world—K2 at 28,251ft (8,611m), Kanchenjunga at 28,169ft (8,585m), and the second of our Asiatic natural wonders, the highest mountain in the world, Mount Everest at 29,032ft (8,848m). Named for Sir George Everest, the British Surveyor-General of India in 1865, the mountain's true name is Chomolungma (Mother Goddess of the Universe) in Tibetan, or Sagarmatha (Goddess of the Sky) in Nepalese. It is part of the Himalayan mountain range that forms the international frontier between Nepal and Tibet (China). Because of the movement of the great tectonic plates under the mountain range, Everest grows taller by a few millimetres every year. It is one of the ultimate challenges for any serious climber and many have lost their lives in the attempt. However, to put all this into perspective, if Mount Everest were to be dropped into the deepest place in the ocean, Challenger Deep in the Mariana Trench, it would be submerged by over 1.25 miles (2km) of water.

Sharing its eastern boundary with Asia (usually considered to be the Ural Mountains) but altogether much smaller is the continent of Europe, although some geographers like to consider it a subcontinent as the western portion of Eurasia. To the north lies the Arctic Ocean, the south the Mediterranean, and the west coast is served by the Atlantic Ocean. It is the second smallest continent and only covers two percent of the Earth's surface. Although Europe contains many unique and fascinating geological features such as the Giant's Causeway in Northern Ireland and the Jurassic coast along the coastal edge of southwest England, none are included in our list.

North America geographically covers almost five percent of Earth's land mass and is the third largest continent. Off the west coast is the Pacific Ocean; off the north lies the Arctic Ocean; to the east is the northern Atlantic Ocean; and the Caribbean Sea lies to the southeast as does Continental South America, to which it is joined by the Isthmus of Panama. This continent contains some a varied landscape—everything from deserts and mountains to vast plains and forests—and climates that encompass everything from permanent ice and snow in the far north of Alaska and Canada to tropical forests in Florida in the extreme southeast.

▲

Mount Everest

▲

The Grand Canyon, Arizona, North America

Arguably the most astonishing natural wonder in the world is the Grand Canyon in Arizona, whose landscape has been formed over the course of millions of years. In the past a high mountain range existed here; over the millennia it was eroded to become a vast plateau; then, as the climate repeatedly changed, oceans came and went leaving successive layers of rock and mineral deposits. About 70 million years ago, the Rocky Mountains were formed and the Colorado River came into being, taking water westward toward the Pacific Ocean. In the process it began to cut its way through the plain, exposing the different layers of rock. About 17 million years ago the Colorado Plateau was forced upward for about five million years. Over time the river changed course, possibly many times, and the combined effect of both titanic forces—the river cutting down and the plateau thrusting up—created deep canyons and passageways. The land was sculpted further by fault lines that developed into side canyons, themselves also eroded, and so the Colorado Canyon was formed.

Our second North American natural wonder is the Niagara Falls on the eastern international boundary between Ontario Province in Canada and the State of New York in the United States. These are actually a series of waterfalls that comprise the collective Niagara Falls. They are the Canadian Horseshoe Falls, separated by Goat Island from the Bridal Veil Falls, and the American Falls. The word "Niagara" comes from the American Indian Iroquois word "Onguiaahra" which means "strait." The rock formations were formed during the last Ice Age 18,000 years ago when the advancing ice sheets gouged out the Great Lakes of North America. When the ice retreated and melted, the lakes filled up with fresh water and even today 20 percent of the world's fresh water lies in the Great Lakes. The escarpment down which the falls flow was created before the development of the Niagara River. The first falls to appear were between Lake Erie and Lake Ontario at Queenston-Lewiston. These then eroded steadily backward through the bedrock and through the process of time the current three sets of falls emerged.

On the north coast of California lies the Redwood National Park that became part of the California World Heritage Site in 1980, only 12 years after its establishment. Within its boundaries lie some of the tallest trees in the world, belonging to the species Sequoia sempervirens, which have lived in this region for some 20 million years. These coastal redwood trees comprise some of the oldest living organisms on Earth, living on average for 600 years, although a Sequoia logged in 1933 was discovered to have been 2,200 years old. Despite this, Sequoias are the fastest growing conifers in North America and will rapidly reach a height of 367ft (122m) with a width at the base of 22ft (7m). The size of these amazing trees is due to the specific climatic conditions found in North California. They live along a fairly

▲

Niagara Falls, Canada

narrow coastal strip that is constantly bathed by the cool moist air drifting in from the Pacific Ocean, which keeps them continually damp even during California's frequent summer droughts and blistering heat.

Oceania comprises the huge island of Australia, New Zealand, Indonesia, and East Timor, plus around 10,000 smaller and even tiny islands scattered across the Pacific Ocean. Much of this vast region has only been explored in relatively recent historic times. The aboriginal peoples of Oceania—and in particular of Australia—have a heritage that goes back for thousands of years, much of which is a mystery to outsiders.

In Australia's Northern Territory, deep in the heart of the outback, lies the world's second largest monolith, a place sacred to the local Aboriginal Pitjantjatjara people who call it Uluru: it is better known in the Western world as Ayers Rock. Now a World Heritage Site and part of Kata Tjuta National Park, the monolith is 986ft (318m) high rising straight out of the surrounding plain. Hidden underground it extends for a further 1.5 miles (2.5km). The circumference is five miles (8km) round. The rock is a massive pebble of coarse-grained sandstone called arkose which approximately 500 million years ago was part of the ocean floor. Despite its colossal size it has eroded substantially over the millennia. The rock got its western name in 1873 after the then Premier of South Australia, Sir Henry Ayers. The rock changes color dramatically thanks to the high percentage of feldspar in the sandstone that reflects the light, especially the red colors of sunrise and sunset. Depending on the time of day and atmospheric conditions it can appear anything from red to blue and even violet.

Although Everest is the highest land-based mountain above sea level on Earth, Mauna Kea (meaning "White Mountain") in Hawaii is actually higher when measured from its base on the mid-Pacific Ocean floor, at 5.6 miles (9km), but only 13,796ft (4,205m) is visible above sea level. Mauna Kea is classified as a dormant volcano and is last known to have erupted 3,500 years ago. However, after being built up in layers over millennia the volcano is now so heavy that it is being crushed into the sea floor and so is slowly diminishing in height.

South America contains about three and a half percent of the Earth's land surface making it the fourth largest continent. The vast Pacific Ocean lies to its west, the South Atlantic to the east, the Southern Ocean to the south, and the Caribbean Sea to the northwest provide all its natural boundaries. The two principal features of the continent are the vast rainforests of Brazil and the long range of the Andes Mountains that stretch virtually all the way along the western side.

The Amazon River is the second longest river in the world after the River Nile in Africa. It rises high in the Andes at Calillona, in Peru, and runs for some 3,920 miles (6,272km)—although this length is much argued over—through much of the northern half of South America to northeastern Brazil. There it enters the sea through a massive delta that is 202 miles (325km) wide. It draws water from thousands of tributaries that account for over 40 percent of the landmass of South

INTRODUCTION

America. The volume of water that the Amazon discharges—ordinarily 4.2 million cubic feet per second—is such that its fresh water is discernible 200 miles (322km) out to sea.

The longest free fall of water in the world is Angel Falls in Canaima National Park, in the Guayana highlands of southwest Venezuela. Known to the local Pemones Native Indians as "Churún Merú," the falls get their western name from American adventurer and bush pilot, Jimmy Angel, who was the first non-local to see this spectacular natural feature in 1933. For a period he had flown with Lindbergh's Flying Circus but on this occasion he was searching for gold ore. The falls plunge down vertically for around 2,421ft (738m) from Auyan-tepui, a huge tabletop mountain known as a "tepui." Canaima became a national park (the seventh largest in the world) in June 1962.

Another notable natural feature in South America is Mount Chimborazo in the Andes range in central Ecuador. It can be argued that Chimborazo is the highest mountain in the world. It rises to 20,561ft (6,267m) and is not even the highest mountain on the continent, but its summit is further from the Earth's core than Mount Everest, even though it is 8,458ft (2,547m) lower. This is because of the Earth's prominent bulge around the equator that makes Chimborazo 1.3 miles (2.1km) farther from the center than the summit of Everest.

Man-made Wonders of the World

The oldest wonders of the world are all natural phenomena, but from the earliest times mankind has been building wondrous structures, in particular temples and places of worship, palaces, and cities. When the Ancient Greeks drew up the list of the Seven Great Wonders of the World they (of course) only included the wonders they knew. Many of our wonders do not date from a single era, but rather have evolved over time to become a remarkable construct. This is particularly true of cities such as Venice, the Forbidden City, Timbuktu, Mecca, and even that remarkable modern mish-mash that is Las Vegas, which is itself a pastiche of many of the wonders of the world all of its own!

When looked at in chronological order our wonders of the world move seemingly randomly from continent to continent; but great civilizations learn from each other through trade and experience, and certainly as cultures become more open their influence is felt over a greater area. For example, during the Napoleonic era French culture in general but particularly in art, fashion, and music, was influential throughout the "civilized" world. Similarly, during the rule of Queen Victoria and the dominance of all things British, that culture was influential in all walks of life across the world. Now the predominant culture in the world is that of the United States, and even once obscure aspects of American life in terms of behavior and food preferences have a profound influence over what can only be termed completely alien cultures.

Many of the pre-twentieth century wonders of the world are immediately identifiable to a particular culture and even a particular historic period, but with the spread of global influence, money, and capabilities, it becomes increasingly harder for the new and prospective wonders of the world to be immediately culturally identifiable. Architects and contractors work anywhere and everywhere around the world taking their work ethics and ethos with them. This makes any given prestige project a multicultural affair and therefore much harder to identify as belonging to a specific place and culture. In "*Wonders of the World*" we are looking at the wonders of the world through a geographical perspective, but there is also the chronological aspect to be considered.

Some of the wonders are so old that their construction date can only be guessed at and given approximately, but it is interesting to discover contemporaneous projects that were being built during much the same era but in different parts of the world. For instance the Great Pyramid at Giza in Egypt was probably built within five hundred years or so of the extraordinary circle of monolithic stones at Stonehenge in England. The sophistication and size of the pyramid dramatically outshines its contemporary—as it remains today—although even now nobody really knows its true purpose. But interestingly, despite their disparities, both were aligned with stars in the galaxy and the Sun and Moon which on a specific day at a particular time would highlight the center of the structure. Such apparent coincidences indicate the importance of the heavens to entirely different early cultures. Other early wonders include the magnificent temple complex of Abu Simbel in Egypt—although in truth almost every Ancient Egyptian site could be included as a wonder of the world. What would the Ancient Greeks have made of the Great Wall of China, constructed on the orders of various Chinese emperors over a period of almost a thousand years and so vast that it can be seen from space? Would they have marveled at its sheer ambition and size or been dismissive of its merely being an especially large fortified wall. Cultural snobs have always existed: interestingly, the Acropolis complex above Athens which includes the magnificent Parthenon did not make the original list of wonders, despite being literally on the doorstep of Antipater of Sidon the putative originator of the list. Was he biased against his neighbor?

Within a hundred or so years of each other the great cities of Petra in Jordan and Teotihuacan in Central America were thriving. Both were long since abandoned and even disappeared from sight as the desert (in the case of Petra) and the jungle (in the case of Teotihuacan) overwhelmed the buildings so much that they entirely disappeared. Both great cities vanished for centuries until rediscovered in recent historic times. They share another similarity, although architecturally and culturally as well as geographically they could hardly be further apart—both civilizations, although rich and important, simply ceased to exist apparently without reason.

▲
Venice, Italy

▲
Stonehenge, England

Archaeologists and historians have struggled to rationalize this dilemma, so far without managing to achieve a consensus.

One of the most astonishing archaeological discoveries of recent times is the army of thousands of terracotta warriors, nobody knows exactly how many as they are still being dug out, in the Mausoleum of the First Qin Emperor in Xi'an, Shaanxi province, China in 1974. These extraordinary life-size figures appear to be individual portraits of the emperor's soldiers and have apparently been taken from life. Nowhere else has anything remotely similar been discovered, but the exciting prospect is that there are more warriors patiently waiting to be found in other Chinese emperor's tombs.

The city of Ephesus in Asia Minor was the capital of proconsular Asia for the Roman Republic and its domain covered western Asia Minor. At its peak it was one of the largest cities in the world and was the home of the Temple of Artemis, one of the original seven wonders. It later became an important center of Christianity where St. Paul worked and finally died at a great age. The remains of the city are now the major tourist attraction in Turkey.

The last of our wonders to be built before the time of Christ is the Wailing Wall in Jerusalem, although as with so many ancient artefacts, the exact date of construction is not known. The Kotel, or al-Buraq, Wall was built as a retaining wall at about the same time as the Jewish Second Temple and Jews have prayed here for two thousand years. Sadly for such a sacred site its ownership is in continual dispute between Muslims and Jews, both of whom consider it to be one of their holiest sites.

The Roman Empire dominated the entire known world and built ambitious structures with such enthusiasm and solidity that their architectural legacy is scattered generously around the Mediterranean and adjoining lands. Of their many outstanding buildings we have chosen the Colosseum in Rome to represent the might of the Romans. The Colosseum—originally called the Amphitheatrum Flavium—was the largest amphitheater built in the Roman world and could contain 50,000 spectators. It was here that the bloody Roman games and gladiatorial combats thrilled the crowds whenever the emperor called a holiday. Although ravaged over the centuries the Colosseum is still an impressive building and enough of it remains for visitors to be able to catch a flavor of its past.

Our next three wonders in chronological order are all of a religious nature. The Vatican in Rome was started soon after the Roman Empire became Christian and continued to be built, improved, and extended by successive popes for hundreds of years. The complex contains the Sistine Chapel that was built in 1473 and decorated by the great Michelangelo. Hagia Sophia in what is now Istanbul has a long and colorful history from its beginnings as an early fourth century church of the Eastern Orthodox version of Christianity. It was converted to a mosque in 1453 when Constantinople (as Istanbul was called then) fell to the Ottoman Turks. Converted again, this time in 1935 to become a museum, it remains one of the great buildings of the world. Mecca is not so much a building as a holy city at the center of which is the al-Masjid al-Haram (the Sacred Mosque), the most holy place on Earth for Muslims. All devout Muslims hope and intend to make at least one journey to Mecca in their lives and every year millions of devotees do so, especially during the

▲
The Terracota Warriors, China

▲
The Colosseum, Italy

INTRODUCTION

▲

Borobudur Temple, Indonesia

▲

A Moai Statue, Easter Island, Chile

Muslim month of Dhu al-Hijjah.

The next two wonders are both remnants of lost civilizations that were all-powerful in their time but became abandoned and all but forgotten and swallowed up by jungle until chance rediscovery by someone from the outside world in the 20th century. In Mexico the lost city of Chichen Itza allows a glimpse into a very different past through it monumental ziggurats and ceremonial temples. Contemporary, but literally a world apart, Borobudur Temple in central Java is not as well known but is a single enormous structure dedicated to Buddha. Also contemporary with Borobudur and also dedicated to Buddha but nevertheless completely different is Kyomizu Temple in Kyoto, Japan that has been in continuous use since its foundation around 798 A.D.

As time moves on, the wonders appear thicker and faster and they also lose the mystery that the earlier wonders possess, with the notable exception of the huge statues—called Moai—on the Polynesian island of Easter Island in the South Pacific Ocean. There are 887 monolithic stone statues that stand around the coastline of the island. Nobody knows for sure what their meaning and purpose were and they will probably remain as one of the great mysteries of archaeology forever.

Many of our remaining wonders are statements of power, economic wealth, and empire. Every civilization not only wants to leave its mark for future generations but also wants to impress contemporaries with its indomitable spirit and might—hence such places as the Forbidden City in China, the Kremlin in Moscow, the beautiful city of Venice that so loved to show its opulence to the world, and the Palace of Versailles created to glorify King Louis XIV, the Sun King, to dazzle and intimidate all who saw or even heard of it.

The early wonders almost exclusively involve religion and the adoration of a god or gods through the creation of an awe-inspiring edifice—churches, temples, mosques. But it is interesting to note that as we hit a more doubting age the last of the religious wonders was created in 1920. This is the huge statue of Christ the Redeemer above the city of Rio de Janeiro in Brazil; since then all the wonders chosen have been secular and almost always highlight commerce in one way or another. The Eiffel Tower was built to glorify French engineering; the Hoover Dam in Colorado was built to provide water and jobs during the Depression but also as a statement of hope and belief in a better and brighter future. Perhaps the greatest futuristic project of them all, Cape Canaveral in Florida, with its ambition of reaching for the stars is the most outward-looking project of them all. Whatever future lies beyond our planet the scientists and astronauts who work there will be involved.

A number of the most recent wonders belong to the entertainment industry that has become globally powerful during the 20th century and will doubtless continue to be so. The business of these wonders concern leisure, although in the case of Las Vegas this is rather hidden by the excesses of vast wealth and vulgarity. Mass entertainment for children—with adults an added bonus—is the not so secret reason for the success of Disneyland in Anaheim, California, one of the first great theme parks of the world. Success, however, was not apparent during its disastrous press preview day on July 17, 1955, when counterfeit tickets made the park over-congested and local roads gridlocked; in blistering heat the asphalt melted, the fountains ran dry, the food ran out, and the press gave the resort a critical pounding. Walt Disney and his executives had to work overtime to get the press back onside and make the theme park a success.

The Race for the Sky

For many people the greatest wonders of the modern world are the high-rise skyscrapers whose very existence is totally dependent on technology. Before the mid-nineteenth century anyone trying to build a tall building was hampered by any number of problems, not least of which was that the base and foundations had to be strong enough to carry the weight of the structure above. Even when reinforced concrete and other engineering innovations were made the problems continued; buildings over six stories were rare because of the practical difficulties.

The designer of one of the early tallest structures, the French engineer Gustave Eiffel, was also one of the first engineers to realize that tall structures had to be built to withstand strong gusts of wind well beyond those normally encountered at ground level. For this reason he deliberately designed his tower in Paris as an open

▲

The Eiffel Tower, Paris, France

▲

The Chrysler Building, New York

lattice of metal trusses, so as to offer as little wind resistance as possible, giving the wind nothing to "push" against.

Buildings became increasingly impractical the higher they were because people had difficulty walking up more than a reasonable number of flights of stairs; also furniture and services had to reach the top. This problem remained insurmountable until several of engineering discoveries were made. The breakthrough that allowed the development of tall habitable buildings was made by William LeBaron Jenney, who discovered a way to use steel beams as the skeleton of a building at a time when all other buildings used bricks both inside and out. This discovery meant that the steel skeleton took the weight of the walls, as opposed to the walls themselves having to be load bearing.

Another crucial breakthrough was the invention of the first power safety elevator by Elisha Otis in 1852. Otis showed off his device at the New York Crystal Palace Exhibition the following year, and in 1856 the first electric passenger elevator was installed in a New York City store. Still other practicalities had to be addressed— namely how to get water up and down a tall building safely with particular regard to the removal of waste water: it couldn't be allowed to just free-fall to the ground. This required the development of sophisticated water pumps.

Once these essentially simple but basic problems were resolved the race to build the tallest building in the world was well and truly on. There are two contenders for the title of being the world's first modern skyscraper, although neither would qualify as such today. They are either the ten-story 138ft (42m) tall brick and steel Home Insurance Building, built in Chicago in 1884–1885 (demolished in 1931) or the 20-story 309ft (94m) New York World Building (also known as the Pulitzer Building), built in New York City in 1890 (demolished in 1955).

However the title of first true skyscraper is usually given as the Woolworth Building in New York City, a true engineering marvel that used cutting-edge technology, not least its caissons which had to be sunk enormously deep to stand on the bedrock of Manhattan. The building was the concept of Frank W. Woolworth as a statement of belief in the Woolworth Corporation and of American architecture, wealth, and importance. In addition he wanted to have the tallest building in the world. Designed by Cass Gilbert and engineered by Gunvald Aus, it was completed in 1931 in the gothic style. It cost in the order of $13.5 million, and went up 59 stories using the latest type of safety elevator to reach a height of 792ft (241m).

Frank W. Woolworth was just the first businessman to use his money and vision to build such a very public statement of intent. Skyscrapers were seen as reflecting the modern age, they shouted prosperity and daring and every entrepreneur wanted his building to be the tallest. In the 1930s the contenders were the Chrysler Building, the Manhattan Company Building, and the Empire State Building. This contest did not concern two rival cities, but rather two rival architects. It was about personal prestige and professional pride and the personalized contest fascinated New Yorkers as first one and then the other gained the advantage. The two men were William Van Alen and Craig Severance, one-time friends and architectural partners but now bitter rivals.

It started when Severance was commissioned in 1929 to design the Manhattan Bank Building in downtown New York. Meanwhile, across Manhattan Van Alen had been commissioned to design and build the Chrysler Building for William Chrysler. The contest became known as the "Great Skyscraper Race" and enthralled New Yorkers and much of the world beyond.

The Woolworth Building lost its title in 1930 to the Bank of Manhattan Trust Building that towered 927ft above Wall Street, earning itself the title of "Crown Jewel of Wall Street." Severance's 71-story steel and limestone former Bank of Manhattan Trust Building is better known these days as the Trump Building. Soon a new word coined in New York—skyscraper—appeared to describe such tall buildings that appeared to literally "scrape" the sky.

The Chrysler Building was the first structure in the world to reach over the magical

1,000ft (319m) height; it remains the tallest brick building in the world and has only recently dropped off the top 20 tallest list. It was constructed at a rapid average of four floors per week and was completed in 1930 with 77 stories served by 32 elevators; it is fully habitable right up to 899ft (274m). When it appeared to be finished it was the same height as the Bank of Manhattan Trust Building, so Severance added another 2ft (0.6m) to his building and claimed the title of the world's tallest. Unknown to him, van Alen had a secret plan and had permission to build a further spire onto the Chrysler Building. This was assembled within the building from five pieces and the outside world knew nothing of it until it appeared on October 23, 1929, when it was hoisted into place, assembled, and riveted in a breathtaking 90 minutes. Made from "Nirosta" stainless steel it added a further 185ft (58.4m) to the Chrysler Building and easily took the title of world's tallest. Although New Yorkers were enraptured by the glittering spire, and van Alen had the satisfaction of a battle won, his employer, Walter Chrysler, refused to pay his fees because he thought van Alen had indulged in some dubious financial shenanigans with some of the contractors. Sadly, van Alen never worked on another major project and perhaps the world has been deprived of another wonderful and original building because of it. A needle was later attached to the spire, taking the building to 1,046ft (319m).

What made these extravagant buildings all the more remarkable was they were built at the height of the great U.S. Depression, the devastating economic slump that saw millions jobless, homeless, and on the brink of starvation. Van Alen and Chrysler thought they had the race won but they only held the title for one brief year. The new champion was the Empire State Building that was built on the site of the former Astoria Hotel. Starting in spring 1930–1931 it thrust upward with 102 stories until it topped out at 1,250ft (381m). Built of Indiana limestone and granite it took 3,000 workers (with very few fatalities, much fewer than expected) a little over 18 months to build, using the latest fast-track construction techniques. It rose at an astonishing average of four and a half stories a week, despite the design being changed 16 times during planning and construction.

The Empire State Building was completed about six weeks ahead of schedule in one year and 45 days—working weekends and holidays. It cost about $41 million, roughly $5 million under budget—thanks to the much lower wages and construction costs during the Depression. More to the point, it was 204ft (62m) taller than the Chrysler Building. A metal plated tower at the summit was built as a dual-purpose zeppelin tethering post and observatory. In fact only one zeppelin moored there because it was immediately apparent that wind speeds at such a height were dangerous; moreover, the brief heyday of the zeppelin was over. The mast stayed in place but mostly redundant until 1951 when a broadcasting antenna was added.

The Empire State Building was officially opened by President Herbert Hoover on May 1, 1931, and held the title of being the tallest building in the world for 41 years until surpassed by Building One of the World Trade Center in 1972. It is so big that it has its own zip code and is currently still in the top ten tallest buildings in the world. From the top viewing area on a clear day it commands an 80-mile view out across Connecticut and Massachusetts, as well as Pennsylvania and New Jersey. New York led the way in the tall buildings race for the first few decades as the city of Chicago imposed strict limits on building heights allowing no more than 40 stories. This was only changed in 1960 when Chicago architects and engineers grabbed their opportunity and turned Chicago into one of the tallest cities on the planet.

Soon other countries joined in the prestige race to build the tallest structures and by the 1930s there were notable skyscrapers in São Paulo and Buenos Aires, as well as in Europe, and in the Far East in Shanghai, Hong Kong, and Kuala Lumpur. In crowded cities across the world where land prices were at a premium, developers quickly realized that their investment in a skyscraper would bring returns not only in prestige but also in the high ratio of rentable floor space per square foot. Where land is expensive, building skyward makes obvious economic sense. City councils in turn encouraged developers to build ever taller: bigger buildings mean more tax dollars for cash-strapped city administrators as well as adding inestimable prestige by presenting their city as being at the cutting edge of economic prosperity and achievement. Nothing shouts money as loudly as a cluster of glittering skyscrapers, as all the newly emerging economies in the Middle and Far East testify.

▲

The Sears Tower, Chicago

The Petronas Towers, Malaysia

In 1972 the Twin Towers of the World Trade Center in Manhattan were built for the Port Authority of New York and New Jersey. The foundations had to be sunk over 70ft (21m) below the landfill ground area to find solid bedrock. The towers took the title of being the world's (two) tallest buildings. One World Trade Center was completed first in 1972 at 1,368ft (417m), followed by Two World Trade Center in 1973 at 1,362ft (415m). The cost was $400 million but despite this it was only two years before the Sears Tower grabbed the title back for Chicago by being built about 100ft (30m) higher.

The Sears Tower was the world's tallest building from 1975 for 22 years until 1997 and remains the tallest building in the United States at 1,450ft (442m) and 110 stories. Sears Tower has the highest occupied floor level in the world, which experts consider to be one of the considerations when the title of tallest is conferred on a building; even today the argument about what constitutes a tall building is a matter of huge contention. The international arbiters on such matters are generally agreed to be the Council on Tall Buildings and Urban Habitat who have drawn up a set of rules, for example that architectural spires can count in a building's height but an antenna does not. The council is made up of specialist engineers, architects, planners, and construction professionals as a forum to discuss "all aspects of the planning, design, construction, and operation of tall buildings and the urban habitat."

Contrary to public expectation that the tallest building in the world is simply the one that measures longest from top to bottom, the council has come up with a number of criteria, in effect to stop "cheating" with the use of high masts and other spurious features. The council has drawn up four categories which put simply (and it does get very complicated) are: the height from sidewalk to the "architectural top" of the building, this specifically excludes antennas but includes towers and spires. Second, the highest occupied floor from sidewalk level; third, to the top of the roof; and fourth and finally, to the top of the pinnacle, i.e. something that is architecturally integral to the overall design of the building.

In 1997 as the Asian economic tiger was making its muscle felt, the astonishing Petronas Towers were built in Kuala Lumpur, Malaysia for the Petronas national oil company. These won the title when counting their huge spires, although not everyone accepts that these qualify for the accolade. Petronas Towers contain 88 floors and are built on foundations that had to be dug 394ft (120m) deep into the ground. The most remarkable feature of the buildings is the 190ft (58m) long skybridge that links the towers on the 41st and 42nd floors, 558ft (170m) above ground level. This vertigo-inspiring feature is open free of charge to the first 1,400 visitors on most days.

The argument over which was the tallest building in the world became academic in 2004 when the $1.8 billion Taipei 101 tower in Taipei, Taiwan was completed and topped out at 1,671ft (509m—over half a kilometer high). It met three of the stated criteria for world's tallest building status by being the tallest to the structural top, the tallest to the roof, and by containing the highest occupied floor. The building's design was inspired by traditional Chinese architecture and resembles a pagoda with the sectioned tower reminiscent of a bamboo stem. In addition it is structured around Chinese numerology and the lucky number "8." A Feng Shui master was consulted about the building but to improve its chances during high winds and earthquakes the building contains a 730-ton (662mt) tuned mass damper that hangs inside the top of the building. Costing $4 million, the welded steel-plate ball's job is to swing like a giant pendulum up to 5ft (1.5m) in any direction and maintain the balance of the building. Taipei 101 sits only 660ft (201m) from a major fault line in the Earth's crust, so not only is this a safety feature but also a crucial selling point for potential tenants.

Despite all its staggering statistics Taipei 101 is only expected to hold the record of being the world's tallest building for a short time. Other even more massive structures are under construction and doubtless even larger ones are in the planning stage. Far from having seen it all, the list of the most amazing Wonders in the World is ever growing.

ABU SIMBEL

▲
The temple of Abu Simbel
IMAGE BY © CARLOS ARGUELLES

▶
Hathor Temple of Queen Nefertari
IMAGE BY © VLADIMIR POMORTZEFF

◀

Sun Temple of Abu Simbel decorated by 20-metre height colossi of Ramses II
IMAGE BY © VLADIMIR POMORTZEFF

This magnificent Ancient Egyptian site was cut out of the rock sometime between 1284 B.C. and 1264 B.C. during the reign of Pharaoh Ramesses II to commemorate his victory at the Battle of Kadesh. The complex consists of two temples. The largest is dedicated to Ra-Harakhty, Ptah, and Amun, the three state deities of Egypt and the frontage features four colossal 66ft (20m) high, seated statues of Ramesses II each sitting on a throne and wearing the double crown of Upper and Lower Egypt. The much smaller figures around his feet represent his family.

The second, smaller temple is dedicated to the goddess Hathor, the goddess of love and beauty, and also to his favorite wife, Nefertari (the living personification of the goddess). The façade is adorned by six statues, four of Ramesses II and two of Nefertari. Despite their massive size, both temples had been swallowed by the desert sands and were only rediscovered in 1813. They were soon dug out and looted.

In the 1960s Lake Nasser was created to provide desperately needed water for the region: this meant swamping the temple and its associated buildings, After an international outcry in the late 1950s a campaign started to save the temples from the rising waters of the Nile. Careful work to dismantle the temples began in 1964 and continued until 1968 when the entire site was relocated just over a mile (200m) back from the Nile onto higher ground. The cost of this enormous project was put at $36 million.

▲
Entrance to the Sun Temple of Abu Simbel
IMAGE BY © VLADIMIR POMORTZEFF

▶

The Hathor Temple built by Ramses II to honour his most loved wife, Nefertari

▲

Heiroglyphs on a wall in Temple of Karnak

◄

Heiroglyphs on a wall in Temple of Amon-Re

▼

Egyption statues kings - Ramesses II, Ramesses III, Tuthmosis III

The Egyptian temple complex of Karnak although badly ruined is one of the most awe inspiring monuments to the ancient gods. Originally called Ipet-isut, meaning "Most Sacred of Places" it is the largest ancient religious site in the world.

During the early New Kingdom the pre-eminent Egyptian god was Amun Re of Thebes and his temple complex was built over a period of some 1,300 years starting in the 16th century BC., and continuing under the auspices of about 30 pharaohs. The Temple of Karnak comprises three main temples, plus smaller enclosed temples, and several outer temples, all located about 2 miles (3km) north of Luxor, on 247 acres (100ha) of land. The three main temples are dedicated to Mut (the mother goddess of the Theban Triad), Montu (the war-god of the Theban Triad and son of Amun-Re and Mut) and Amun Re (the chief god of the Theban Triad), and all are enclosed by enormous brick walls to keep away prying eyes.

The Temple of Amun is by far the largest at the site and is situated at the heart of the entire complex. Next to it inside the enclosure wall is the Temple of Ptah, with the Temple of Mut to the south, and the Temple of Montu to the north. In addition there are a number of smaller temples and chapels across the site, such as the temples of Osiris Hek-Djet and Khonsu Opet. One of the most spectacular sights are the avenues of ram-headed sphinxes flanking the way between the three main temples.

The ruins of the Temple of Amenhotep IV have long since been dismantled but once stood to the east of the main complex. It was destroyed after the death of its builder, and its full extent and lay-out is unknown.

▲

Entrance to the temple of Amon-Re

NILE

◀

The Nile crocodile : crocdylus niloticus

▶

Fellukahs on the Nile

▲

Buildings on the Nile

▼

A riverside scene on the River Nile

▲

The bank of Nile

The Nile is the longest river in the world (although when all the tributaries are included some give this accolade to the Amazon). Much of Egypt is arid desert, making the Nile particularly important to the peoples living alongside. Since ancient times the waters have determined the economy of Egypt: without its annual inundation (flood), Egypt remains dry. Almost 85 percent of the flood originates from the summer rains in Ethiopia—if the rains fail there, there is no flood.

The name Nile comes from the Greek word *Neilos* meaning a river valley: another Greek word for this was *Aigyptos* from which the name Egypt comes. The two principal components of the Nile are the White Nile that rises in equatorial East Africa and the Blue Nile that rises in the highlands of Ethiopia: both rivers are formed on the western side of the Great Rift Valley that cuts through Africa. The two great rivers meet at the Sudanese city of Khartoum.

For many years the source of the Nile was unknown. This great mystery was solved in 1858 when John Hanning Speke showed that the source of the (White) Nile was Lake Victoria in central East Africa. Subsequently, Lake Victoria has been revealed to be fed by significant rivers, in particular a stream that starts in Rwanda. It becomes the White Nile or Bahr al Abyad—named for the pale clay particles suspended in its waters—where it meets the Bahr el Ghazal in Sudan. From there, the river flows to Khartoum where it joins the Blue Nile to form the River Nile.

The Blue Nile—known as Bahr al Azraq in Sudan and Abbay in Ethiopia—starts at Lake Tana in the Ethiopian highlands and flows for about 850 miles (1,400km) to Khartoum.

▶

Temple of Philae, on the bank of the Nile

TABLE MOUNTAIN

Table Mountain is a mountain in the Western Cape, South Africa, overlooking the greater Cape Town area. It forms part of the Table Mountain National Park and is flanked by Devil's Peak to the east and by Lion's Head and Signal Hill to the north. Table mountain is a famous landmark and tourist attraction in Cape Town, with many visitors using the cableway to take a ride to the top. The mountain is named for its flat top which is often covered by cloud, forming the "table cloth". It stands 1,086 m above sea level at its peak and the main face is approximately 3 km from side to side.

The mountain's highest point is at Maclear's Beacon, named for a stone cairn built there in 1865 by Sir Thomas Maclear for trigonometrical survey. It is 1,086 m (3,563 ft) above sea level and is the highest point of the plateau at the summit, about 19 m above the cable station.

Most major features of the mountain are named. The cliff immediately below the cable station is called Arrow Buttress and the area at the opposite end of the main cliff is called "Ledges". About a third of the way along from Arrow Buttress is a deep and partially hidden ravine called Platteklip Gorge (lit. "Flat Stone Gorge"), which provides an easy ascent to the summit and was the route taken by Antonio de Saldanha on the first recorded ascent of the mountain (see History). A famous and dangerous feature is Carrell's ledge, which winds its narrow way across the face of a vast and sheer drop to the south of Devil's Peak. At one point the ledge is less than 200 mm wide.

Table Mountain is in the unique position of being the only terrestrial feature to give its name to a constellation — Mensa, meaning The Table. The constellation is seen in the Southern Hemisphere, below Orion, around midnight in mid-July. It was named by the French astronomer Nicolas de Lacaille during his stay at the Cape in the mid eighteenth century.

PYRAMIDS OF GIZA

◀

The Great Pyramids of Giza

▶

The Sphinx, with one of the pyramids in the background.

▲

The head of the Sphinx

▲

Pyramid ruins at Giza

▼

Close up showing the stonework of a pyramid at Giza

The rocky desert plateau at Giza near the ancient city of Memphis was used by the Ancient Egyptians as the necropolis for enormous royal tombs known as pyramids. At Giza there are three large pyramids built for the Fourth Dynasty kings Khufu (or Cheops), Khafre (or Chephren) and Menkaure (or Mykerinus). The largest is the Pyramid of Khufu (also called the Great Pyramid) and is the only surviving member of the original Seven Wonders of the World. It was originally 479ft (146m) high until it was robbed of its outer casing and capstone. The Pyramid of Khafre, although smaller, appears as big because it is on higher ground, and the third and much smaller pyramid belongs to Menkaure. In addition there are a number of smaller "queen" pyramids, causeways, mortuary temples, and numerous other minor tombs for members of the royal family and important officials. Sadly all these magnificent tombs and buildings were stripped of their valuables in antiquity, probably within a few years of being used.

Also at the complex is the mysterious Great Sphinx. It is carved out of a limestone outcrop, although the head is carved from a naturally occurring outcrop of harder stone. It is part of the funerary complex of Khafre, whose face it probably wears, but the Sphinx is almost certainly far older. It has the body of a lion but the nose and royal uraeus (the sacred serpent) on the headdress became lost long ago. The Sphinx is 240ft (73m) long and 66ft (20m) high and orientated due east. For somewhere around five thousand years the Sphinx has been almost completely smothered by the desert sands.

These ancient sites in Giza together with others in the Memphis area—at Saqqara, Dahshur, Abu Ruwaysh, and Abusir—were collectively declared a World Heritage site in 1979.

▲

The Great Sphinx with Great Pyramid of Khufu in background

SERENGETI

◄

The Ngorongoro conservation area

►

Wildebeast migration

►

The Ngorongoro Crater

Serengeti National Park is a UNESCO World Heritage Site in northern Tanzania, East Africa. It covers 5,700sq miles (14, 763sq km) of vast grassy rolling plains that teem with wildlife. The Serengeti National Park is part of the greater Serengeti ecosystem along with the Ngorongoro Conservation Area, the Maswa Game Reserve, the Loliondo, Grumeti, and Ikorongo Controlled Areas, and in the north is contiguous with the Masai Mara National Reserve in Kenya. For the Masai tribespeople who have lived here for millennia it is called *Siringitu*, meaning "the place where the land moves on forever."

An estimated three million large mammals roam the plains, in particular lions, leopards, elephants, rhinoceroses, and Cape buffalo. Other important species include hyenas, cheetahs, zebras, gazelles, giraffes, and birds of prey such as fish eagles and vultures as well as nearly 500 different species of bird including storks and flamingos and plenty of insects and reptiles and snakes.

Each year the Serengeti sees great animal migrations: every October and November for the short rainy season over a million wildebeest and around 200,000 zebras move from the northern hills to the southern plains to enjoy the newly sprouted grasslands. Then, after the long rainy season that starts in April and ends in June the same vast migration occurs in reverse. The Serengeti National Park has become a great tourist attraction and such colossal animal migrations are one of the great highlights.

This area is one of the earliest cradles of mankind and in nearby Oldupai Gorge, many of the oldest hominid fossils—almost two million years old—and artefacts have been found.

▲

The Manayara lake area

►

A Wildebeast at the Ngorongoro Crater

◄

Sparse trees on the Serengeti plain.

VICTORIA FALLS

The Victoria waterfall

▶ *The Zimbabwe side of the Victoria falls*

▲ *The top of the Victoria Falls*

Victoria Falls—or more properly, *Mosi-oa-Tunya* (the "Smoke that Thunders" as local peoples call it—is one of the most spectacular waterfalls in the world and a UNESCO World Heritage Site. The falls straddle the border between Zambia and Zimbabwe where the Zambezi river plunges into a deep and narrow chasm caused by a fault line in the earth. The falls were named by the Scottish explorer David Livingstone—the first outsider to see the falls in 1855—to honor his monarch, Queen Victoria.

The great Zambezi flows from its source in the marshy bogs of northwestern Zambia for 1,600 miles (2,574km) to the Indian Ocean through Angola, along the border of Namibia, through Botswana, Zambia, Zimbabwe, and Mozambique. About halfway along its course the Zambezi spreads out over a level sheet of basalt before it plunges over Victoria Falls into a deep chasm about 400ft (120m) wide. This is the point at which the Upper Zambezi ends and the Middle Zambezi begins.

The falls are almost a mile wide (1.7km), and on either side drop from about 262ft (80m), while in the center they rise to about 344ft (105m). The local name *Mosi-oa-Tunya* refers to the roaring volume of the water and to the huge amount of mist and spray created by the drop. This can rise as much as a mile into the air and be seen from as far away as 25 miles (40km) on a clear day.

Victoria Falls are now part of two national parks, Mosi-oa-Tunya National Park in Zambia and Victoria Falls National Park in Zimbabwe, and are one of the major tourist destinations in Africa.

◀ *Aerial view of the Victoria Falls*

▲ *Victoria waterfall fed by the mighty Zambezi river*

ANGKOR WAT

◀
The temple of Angkor on the Siem Reap river

▶

View from an air baloon of the Angkor Wat Temple

▲

Angkor Wat at dusk

The Cambodian city of Angkor in the northwest of the country was the capital of the Ancient Khmer Empire founded around the ninth century by King Jayavarman II. Within the city lies the biggest tourist attraction in Cambodia and a symbol on the national flag—the temple of Angkor Wat. The temple was built in the early twelfth century by King Suryavarman II (who reigned 1131–1150 A.D.) as his state temple and uniquely it has remained an important religious center, Hindu then Buddhist, since its foundation.

Angkor Wat is built and designed in the high classical Khmer style of architecture to represent Mount Meru, the home of the Hindu gods and center of the Hindu universe. Dedicated to the Hindu god Vishnu, the temple took 30 years to build. It is designed like a mountain, orientated to the west for reasons that scholars cannot agree on.

The temple complex covers around 200 acres (81 hectares). The building is encircled by a moat and an outer wall a little over 2 miles (3.6km) long which symbolize the ocean and surrounding mountain ranges respectively. Inside this lie three rectangular concentric galleries each raised above the next. Right in the center sit five towers arranged like the spots on a die (four at the corners and one in the middle) and symbolizing the five peaks of Mount Meru. The entire temple is elaborately decorated and carved and contains the longest continuous bas-reliefs in the world. These run along the outer gallery walls telling stories from Hindu mythology. The common people were only allowed into the lowest level of the temple.

When the Ancient Khmer Empire declined Angkor Wat became a Buddhist temple and has remained one ever since. The entire city of Angkor became a World Heritage Site in 1992.

▲

One of the entrances to the temple of Angkor

◀

Giant sculpture in the Angkor temple complex

▶

Relief decoration on the outside of the temple of Angkor

FORBIDDEN CITY

The Forbidden City was the imperial palace for 24 Chinese emperors and is located in the heart of ancient Beijing on the northern edge of Tiananmen Square. It is a vast complex that contains some 800 buildings with over 8,600 rooms and many fabulous treasures.

Construction of the Forbidden City started during the Ming Dynasty in 1406 and took some 200,000 men 14 years to build. It was completed in 1420 and occupied from then by a succession of 14 Ming Dynasty emperors until 1644, when a peasant revolt led by Li Zicheng occupied the city and ended their dynasty. The following ten emperors of the Qing Dynasty lived in the Forbidden City which they used as their center of government. The only foreign occupation of the city during its five centuries as the imperial palace occurred during the Second Anglo-Chinese Opium War (1857–1860) when the British forced their way in and occupied the Forbidden City in 1860.

In 1912 the last Emperor of China, Pu Yi, was forced to abdicate and the Forbidden City lost its position as the most important political center in China. During the upheavals of the 1940s many of the most valuable artifacts from the Forbidden City were moved away for safekeeping—particularly from the Japanese—until finally in 1947 Chiang Kai-shek ordered their removal to Taiwan where they were placed in the National Palace Museum in Taipei.

The Imperial Palace of the Ming and Qing Dynasties was declared a World Heritage Site in 1987. The Palace Museum inside the Forbidden City is one of Beijing's major attractions.

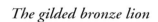

▲
The stairs at the forbidden City

▼
The gilded bronze lion

GREAT WALL OF CHINA

The longest and most extensive construction in the world, the Great Wall of China extends for over 4,500 miles (7,242km), although estimates vary greatly, across north and north-central China. It was begun sometime between 770 B.C. and 476 B.C. during the Zhou Dynasty as a military fortification against border tribes. Then, to keep out northern nomadic invaders three states, the Yan, Zhao, and Qin built their own wall defenses. These were joined to become the Great Wall on orders from Emperor Qin Shi Huangdi, the emperor who unified China in 214 B.C. This first great wall took around ten years to complete.

Succeeding dynasties lengthened and strengthened the wall, in particular the Ming Dynasty that renovated the wall 18 times as the northern nomads—particularly the Mongols and Turkic nomadic tribes—increased in strength and threat. By the time construction finished at the beginning of the 17th century the wall had reached a length of some 4,163 miles (6,700km) and crossed plains, deserts, mountains, and plateaux from east to west across northern China.

The wall was built with regular watchtowers and signal towers and, where necessary, moats. During the Ming Dynasty it was made more sophisticated with the use of garrison towns, blockhouses, passes, additional walls, and even more beacons and watchtowers. The height of the wall averaged 33ft (10m) and the width 16ft (5m). It was made from local materials and resources and built by huge numbers of soldiers, prisoners, and conscripted locals. The work was dangerous as hostile raiding parties enjoyed attacking the workers—this earned the wall the title "the long graveyard." Most of the wall that remains today dates from the Ming Dynasty, especially that around Beijing.

▲ *The Great Wall in early morning mist* ▼ *Staircase leading up to a guard tower*

▲
View looking down into a valley that the Wall crosses

TERRACOTTA WARRIORS

▲
Close up of the Terracota Warriors

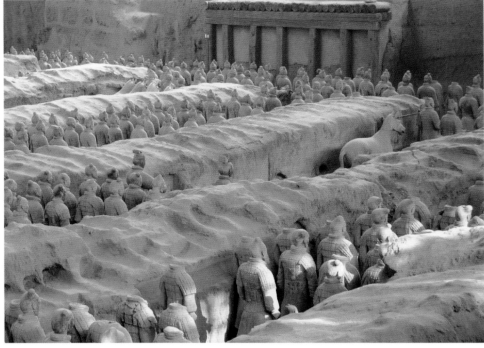

▲
The Terracota army, showing the excavation

▶
The Terracota Warriors
IMAGE BY © RAFAEL MARTIN-GAITERO

The Terra-cotta Army is an astonishing archaeological find discovered in 1974 near Xi'an in Shaanxi Province, China. Farmers digging for a well found a number of obviously ancient pottery shards—and this insignificant find led to the army. There are about 8,099 (they have not all been unearthed yet) life-size terra-cotta figures of soldiers and horses—the Imperial Guard—from the mausoleum of the first Qin Emperor Qin Shi Huang of around 210–209 B.C.

Qin Shi Huang came to the throne age 13 in 246 B.C. and work soon started on his mausoleum which took 11 years to build. The army was assembled to protect the Emperor in the afterlife and as such they were buried in battle order, about a mile (1.5km) east of his tomb, facing enemy territory, booted and suited and ready to come to his aid when called.

The different sections of the army were buried in three separate pits. The largest section with the biggest pit contains the infantry; the cavalry occupy the second pit, while the officers station the third. A fourth pit was intended to contain the supply train but it was never prepared. Each warrior is individually modeled and facially and physically different from his neighbor, so much so that experts believe that the models are life portraits of the real Imperial Guardsmen.

Unfortunately, because of extensive damage to the rooms all the statues have been shattered into pieces and their excavation is a long and painstaking process. The process of unearthing, identifying and reassembling the statues will continue for many years yet. The army can now be seen in Museum of Qin Terra-Cotta Warriors and Horses at Xian, China.

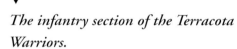

▼
The infantry section of the Terracota Warriors.

▲
The cavalry section of the Terracota Warriors

THREE GORGES DAM

▲
Upstream side of the Three Gorges dam

▶
Satellite view of the Three Gorges dam

One of the biggest engineering projects ever as well as one of the most controversial has been the damming of the River Yangtze in Hubei province, China. Three Gorges Dam will be the largest hydroelectric dam in the world when it becomes fully operational in 2009. The construction is also unofficially estimated to be the costliest building project ever, at $100 billion, although the Chinese refute this. The original plan for the Three Gorges Dam was approved by the National People's Congress in 1992, but in 1997 the plans were changed to maximize the dam's power output, meaning that more land would be flooded and thousands more people displaced. The dam is needed to provide east coast China with electricity and was expected to fulfill 10 percent of China'a electricity needs by 2009, but that figure has been reduced to only 3 percent due to China's booming industries and growing economy. 26 hydro turbines will generate up to 18 gigawatts of electricity, roughly the equivalent of eighteen coal power stations.

The waters will submerge valuable arable land and the homes of well over a million people in the beautiful Three Gorges area between the cities of Yichang, Hubei, and Fuling, and of Chongqing Municipality. When finished the reservoir will be 370 miles (600km) long and inundate some 1,300 archeological sites that contain remnants of the homeland of the ancient Ba peoples who settled in the region more than 4,000 years ago. Some cultural and historical relics are being moved to higher ground but most will disappear. The reservoir started filling on June 1, 2003 and will take years to fill completely. Valuable wildlife habitats will disappear as will many endangered species already on the verge of extinction such as the Chinese Paddlefish and the Chinese River Dolphin.

◀
The Yangtze river

▶
Construction site on the Three Gorges Dam

◀
Ship locks for river traffic to bypass the dam

BURGH AL ARAB

◄ *The Burgh Al Arab atrium*　　　► *The Burgh Al Arab Hotel*

The tallest hotel in the world and one of the most exclusive Burj al-Arab in Dubai in the United Arab Emirates stands on its own artificial island surrounded by the Persian Gulf and sits 919ft (280m) from the shore. The hotel rises up in a great sail shape (actually that of the local Arabian dhows) 1,053ft (321m) into the air and is connected to the mainland by a private equally dramatic curving bridge.

The hotel took five years to build and opened to guests for the first time on December 1, 1999. The hotel contains every conceivable luxury including the inevitable helipad on the roof. Some of its remarkable features include the tallest atrium lobby in the world at 590ft (180m) the volume of which could accommodate the Dubai World Trade Center building, the tallest building in Dubai from the late 1970s to the late 1990s. The outer beachward wall of the atrium is made of a woven, Teflon-coated fiberglass cloth.

At the top of Burj al-Arab visitors can enjoy the spectacular views from the Al Muntaha (meaning Ultimate in Arabic) restaurant which sits supported by a cantilever out over the ocean. The rooms are huge making it one of the most expensive hotels in the world to stay in. There are 202 duplex suites which are anything between 1,819sq ft (169sq m) to 8,396sq ft (780sq m) in size depending on how much you want to pay.

The cost of building the hotel and then furnishing to the highest specification was astronomical and has never been publicly revealed.

◄

The conference room

►

A magnificent staircase in a suite

▼

The Al Farak ballroom

HONG KONG AIRPORT

Known locally as Chek Lap Kok Airport, Hong Kong International Airport (HKIA) opened in 1998 and is the principal airport serving Hong Kong. The airport is built on Chek Lap Kok Island just off the north shore of Lantau Island. It was built to replace the former Hong Kong International Airport (Kai Tak), located in the heavily built up Kowloon City area. Its single runway extended into Kowloon Bay and the airport was renowned for its hair-raising arrivals and departures between the high-rise buildings.

Chek Lap Kok was built on an artificial island with land reclaimed from leveling Chek Lap Kok and Lam Chau islands. The artificial island is almost 5sq miles (12.48sq km) and added almost one percent to Hong Kong's surface area. It is connected to the northern side of Lantau Island near the newly expanded village of Tung Chung. In addition to the airport an entire new infrastructure system had to be installed to facilitate ground traffic movement to and from the terminal. This involved the construction of new road and rail links, plus numerous bridges and tunnels as well as major land reclamation projects in both Kowloon and Hong Kong. The airport took six years and cost $20 billion to build. The architects were Foster and Partners and the airport opened for commercial operations on July 6, 1998. HKIA airport serves mainland China and Asia as well as being important as a regional trans-shipment center. Services operate around the clock and can handle 45 million passengers and three million tonnes of cargo a year. It is the main hub for Cathay Pacific and Dragonair as well as a number of smaller airlines.

AJANTA CAVES

In Ajintha village in the Aurangabad district of Maharashtra State, India lie the remarkable Ajanta Caves. The caves are hidden deep under the trees of a rugged horseshoe-shaped ravine and were carved by Buddhist monks in the second and first centuries B.C. 400 years later, during the Gupta period (fifth and sixth centuries A.D.) more richly decorated caves were added to the assembly. The cave complex was lived in continuously from 200 B.C. to about 650 A.D. when the site was abandoned in favor of the caves at Ellora.

There are 30 caves in total cut into the steep south side of the ravine and vary from 35 to 110ft (11-33m) above the bed of the Waghora river. Some of the caves are unfinished. Five caves are *chaitya-grihas* (prayer halls) and the rest are *viharas* (monasteries) which are thought to have been occupied by around 200 monks and artisans. Originally each of the caves was reached by its own staircase leading up from the river below.

The two phases of cave construction coincide with the two schools of Buddhism: the older Hinayana school only showed the Buddha in symbols, as a stupa, a throne, or set of footprints, while the later Mahayana sect showed Buddha in human form. The artworks are painted in the tempera technique on a ground of mud plaster. They show religious scenes, particularly of Buddha and stories from his life and previous lives (the bodhisattvas) as told in the allegorical Jataka tales.

After being largely forgotten the caves were rediscovered in 1819 by some British officers hunting in the forest of western Deccan when they spotted a tiger silhouetted against a dark cave mouth high up a cliff. Upon investigation they discovered a series of elaborated carved and decorated caves.

◀

The Ajanta Caves as seen from a walkway

▲

One of the entances to the Ajanta Caves

TAJ MAHAL

▲
View from the gardens of the Taj Mahal

▶
The riverside of the Taj Mahal

One of the most romantic buildings in the world, it is also the finest example of Mughal architecture. The Taj Mahal is the mausoleum for Arjumand Bano Begum, (better known as Mumtaz Mahal), the beloved wife of Mughal Emperor Shah Jahan. Mumtaz was the love of his life and his constant companion, she had already given Shah Jahan thirteen children when she died during her fourteenth labor. The Shah was reportedly desolate at the loss and eventually consoled himself with the construction of her magnificent mausoleum. He had already created the gardens and palaces of Shalimar for Mumtaz.

The Taj Mahal was built between 1631 and 1648 by 20,000 skilled builders and craftsmen from Delhi, Qannauj, Lahore, and Multan. In addition specialist craftsmen were called in from Baghdad, Shiraz, and Bukhara. The building cost somewhere around 32 million rupees and nearly bankrupted India.

The Taj was designed by Ustad 'Isa, one of the greatest Islamic architects whose design used interlocking arabesques with self-replicating geometry to give symmetry to the building. It is mainly built of white marble and stands on a raised platform 186ft (57m) square. The high central dome is flanked by four smaller domed chambers and four slender minarets. The entire building is intricately decorated and carved with passages from the Koran and inlaid with precious gems.

The Taj sits behind a *charbagh* (a formal Persian-inspired Mughal garden divided into four equal parts) of 3,229sq ft (300sq m); this contains symmetrical pathways, avenues of trees, flowerbeds, fruit trees, fountains, streams and reflecting pools. Each garden quarter is divided into 16 flower-filled beds, with a raised marble water tank at the center. The whole is a representation of the gardens of Paradise.

▲
Taj Mahal minarete

▼
The gardens of the Taj Mahal

▶
Detail of the Taj Mahal

BOROBUDUR TEMPLE

◀

Stupas at the top of Borobudur

▶

Sunrise over Borobudur Temple

▲

Sand stone carving on Borobudur Wall

▼

Buddha Statue at Borobudur

The largest Buddhist monument on earth is the Borobudur in Central Java. A stupa in the Mahayana tradition, it was built as a replica of the universe probably between 750 and 850 B.C. by the Javanese rulers of the Sailendra dynasties. For 150 years it was the spiritual center of Buddhism in Java. Then for centuries it was "lost" to the wider world until rediscovered by Sir Thomas Stanford Raffles in 1814, by which time it was almost completely buried and in ruins. Restoration started in 1905 and was continued intermittently until 1983.

Borobudur takes the form of a stepped pyramid that rises in six rectangular stories, then three circular terraces topped with a central stupa which is encircled by 72 smaller stupas. These circular structures represent eternity without beginning and without end, and show a tranquil and formless world. Seen from above it looks like either a giant mandala or a lotus, the sacred flower of Buddha that symbolically shows the path of the bodhisattva from samsara to nirvana.

Borobudur was designed to reflect Buddhist cosmology that divides the universe into three separate levels: *Kamadhatu*—the world of desire, *Ruphadhatu*—the world of forms, and *Arupadhatu*—the world of formlessness. To achieve enlightenment a supplicant walks in an anticlockwise direction for 2 miles (3km) while meditating or chanting, through elaborately carved stone galleries describing the life of Buddha Shakyamuni and the principles of his teaching.

In its entirety the Borobudur contains 1,212 carved panels and originally held 504 statues of Buddha, although many are now damaged or missing. Each of these shows a *mudra* (hand gesture) indicating one of five directions: the center shows the gesture of teaching; east, calling the earth to witness; south, the position of blessing; west, the gesture of meditation; and north, the sign of fearlessness.

▲

The Borobudur Temple

WAILING WALL

▲ *Sunrise over the wailing wall*   ▶ *Wailing wall and temple mount*

The Wailing Wall, also called the Western Wall, the Kotel, or the al-Buraq Wall, is a retaining wall dating from the time of the Jewish Second Temple, the most sacred building in Judaism where Jews have prayed for two thousand years. The site is holy to three of the major religions of the world—Judaism, Christianity, and Islam—and ownership has been disputed down the centuries.

The First Temple (also known as Solomon's Temple) was built around 10 B.C. on Temple Mount, Jerusalem and destroyed by the Babylonians in 586 B.C. The Second Temple was destroyed after about four centuries by the Roman Empire in 70 A.D. during the First Jewish-Roman War after Herod the Great had extended the holy area by building vast retaining walls around Mount Moriah.

According to ancient Jewish texts, when the Temple was destroyed by Emperor Titus's soldiers only the western wall, part of the outer courtyard, remained standing. Tradition states that this was left as a deliberate message to the Jews as a potent reminder that Rome had vanquished Judea. The Jews, however, believe that the wall's survival is proof of God's promise that some part of the holy temple would remain as a sign of his unbroken bond with the Jewish people. Southern and eastern sections of wall remain but the Western Wall is believed to be the only piece of the temple and so is the holiest.

Devotional Jews pray three times a day for God to return to the Land of Israel, unite all Jewish exiles, and rebuild the Third Temple and so bring about the messianic era with the arrival of Mashiach (the Jewish Messiah). Traditionally, Jews place a prayer written on a small piece of paper into a crack in the wall.

▲ *The old city of Jerusalem*   ▼ *Old city of david in jerusalem*

▶

Western Wall

AKASHI-KAIKYO BRIDGE

▲
The Bridge in fog

▶
The Akashi-Kaikyo bridge with Kobe in the background

The Akashi Strait in Japan is a notoriously dangerous stretch of water that is an important highway and international shipping lane between Kobe and Awaji Island. Traditionally ferries carry commuters, passengers, and goods between the two but the waters have claimed many lives as the area is prone to severe typhoons. However it became a national imperative to build a bridge across the strait when 168 children were drowned during a storm in 1955. Work eventually started in May 1988 to build a suspension bridge across the Akashi Strait to link Maiko in Kobe and Iwaya on Awaji Island as part of the Honshu-Shikoku Highway.

Pearl Bridge as it is also called, has the longest bridge span in the world in its 6,532ft (1,991m) central span; this was necessary as the Strait is an international waterway and as such required a 5,921ft (1,500m) shipping lane. The side spans are each 3,150ft (960m) across.

The bridge opened for traffic on April 5, 1998. The bridge holds six lanes of traffic and is designed to withstand wind speeds of up to 178mph (286km/h), raging sea currents, and earthquakes measuring up to 8.5 on the Richter scale. In fact the central span was originally 3ft (1m) shorter but was stretched by the Kobe earthquake on January 17, 1995. The bridge also contains hanging weights that operate at the frequency of the bridge to dampen down motion caused by traffic, wind, sea, and weather.

Such technology made the bridge enormously expensive to build, an estimated ¥500 billion ($5 billion), and necessitates the charging of a toll to recoup the costs. However, the charge is so high that many prefer to use the considerably cheaper ferries instead.

▲
The bridge at dusk

▼
The impressive span of the bridge

▲
Mount Fuji behind a lake with blossom trees

▼
A Cherry shrimp farm

▲
Mount fuji in the background of the pacific coast

▶
Mount Fuji rises in the distance

The most iconic image of Japan is of Mount Fuji, the symmetrically beautiful, snow-capped volcano near the Pacific coast of central Honshu, which on a clear day it can be seen as far away as Tokyo. The image of the mountain appears in Japanese art and culture, and is especially beautifully portrayed by Japanese print artists. Japan's two major religions, Buddhism and Shinto, regard Fuji as sacred and encourage their believers to climb the sacred mountain: thousands accordingly climb it each year. The name Fuji probably translates from the indigenous Ainu word meaning "deity of fire" and many legends are linked to the mountain.

Mount Fuji is located on the boundary between the prefectures of Shizuoka and Yamanashi, to the west of Tokyo. Fuji-Hakone-Izu National Park has been created around the sacred mountain and also contains five beautiful lakes, Lake Kawaguchiko, Lake Yamanakako, Lake Saiko, Lake Motosuko and Lake Shojiko. Fuji is 12,388ft (3,776m) high and is the tallest mountain in Japan. The volcano appears where the Eurasian Plate, the Okhotsk Plate, and the Philippine Plate collide. It is a composite volcano—this means it has been built up in layer after layer of lava—and is currently classified as active, although of low risk. Mount Fuji was created in four distinct phases: Sen-komitake is the deep core composed of a type of andesite; Komitake Fuji is a basalt layer formed several hundred thousand years ago. Then, around 100,000 years ago, Old Fuji was formed over the top; finally the top layer, New Fuji was formed about 10,000 years ago.

The most recent eruption was in 1707 during the Edo period, when it lasted for 16 days and blew a new crater and a second peak formed halfway down the side.

▲
Mount Fuji rising above a tea plantation

KYOMIZU TEMPLE

Otowasan Kiyomizudera in eastern Kyoto is a Buddhist temple which dates back to around 780 A.D., although the present wooden building dates from 1633. The name *kiyoi mizu* means "pure water" in reference to the nearby waterfall. The waterfall itself is beneath the main hall and is called *Otowa-no-taki* and is composed of three channels of water that fall into a pond—these confer health, longevity, and success in scholarship. Visitors use metal cups to catch the stream so they can share its therapeutic benefits. A popular pastime is to take the water to a nearby tea shop where they will make a brew for you.

Kiyomizudera is the name of several Buddhist temples but it is this one in Kyoto high up on Sound-of-Feathers Mountain that is most revered. It is reached up a twisting street lined with restaurants, ryokan (inns), and souvenir shops. The main hall of the temple—which belongs to the Japanese Buddhist Hosso sect—is distinctive for its huge veranda that juts out over the hillside and is supported by hundreds of wooden pillars and from where there are magnificent views out over Kyoto. The temple has been much copied by other lesser temples all over Japan. Within the temple grounds lie other shrines, in particular that of Jishu-jinja, which is dedicated to Okuninushino-Mikoto, a god of love and good marriages. A popular custom here for aspiring lovers (whether or not they have a partner) is to walk with eyes shut between a pair of "love stones" that are 60ft (18m) apart. A successful traverse is taken as a good omen.

In 1994 the Otowasan Kiyomizudera became a World Heritage Site.

PETRA

▲ The famous view through the gorge of El Kazneh

▲ Dwellings carved into the rock at Wadi Musa

▶ Entrance to Petra

This ancient city carved out of rose-colored sandstone lies in Jordan and is known locally as Wadi Musa, the name of the stream that flows through it; the name Petra comes from the Greek, meaning rock. This naturally fortified city is located in the eastern flank of the Wadi Araba, a huge cleft valley that runs between the Gulf of Arabia and the Dead Sea. Petra was the capital of the Nabataean civilization and in ancient times was an important trading center controlling the caravan routes linking the Persian Gulf with Gaza in the west, Damascus and Basra in the north, to Aqaba and Leuce Come on the Red Sea. This trade brought great wealth to Petra until the rise of its rival Palmyra.

From the east the entrance to Petra is protected between high cliff walls before opening out into a plain where the city was built. There are some 800 structures within Petra: the most famous of these is the Khazneh el-Farun (Pharaoh's Treasury), with a two-story facade topped with a Hellenistic split pediment. At the base of the mountain en-Nejr lies a massive theater from where the surrounding cliff tombs have been cut into the deeply fissured rock face.

Petra was occupied by the Edomites and by the Arab Nabataeans who had their capital there from the fourth century B.C. until the Roman occupation in 106 A.D. when it became part of Arabia Petraea. Some scholars think that the city of Sela in the Bible (2 Kings 14.7) is Petra. It was certainly an early seat of Christianity until it was captured by the Muslims in the seventh century. Later in the 12th Petra was taken for a time by the crusaders. The city remained lost to the outside world until rediscovered by Johan Burckhardt in 1812.

▼ The great city of Petra

▲ Interior of El Kazneh

PETRONAS TOWERS

Between 1998 and October 2003 the Petronas Twin Towers in Kuala Lumpur, Malaysia, were the tallest buildings in the world. They remain the tallest twin buildings and will always be the tallest structures built in the 20th century. Designed by the Argentinean architect César Pelli, the towers each have 88 floors of reinforced concrete with 16,000 windows. The towers have a stainless steel and glass facade and are joined on the 42nd floor by a flexible skybridge. When the tall spire is counted the towers reach 1,483ft (452m). Pelli's design uses Islamic motifs an important aspect of Malaysia's Muslim heritage and each tower's floor plan forms an eight-pointed star, a traditional Malaysian Islamic pattern. It takes 90 seconds to travel from the basement parking lot to the top of each tower.

The towers are built on the old Kuala Lumpur race track and the foundations had to be drilled down 394ft (120m) to find the bedrock and then backfilled with colossal amounts of concrete. In fact the construction of the towers became a race between the two different contractors: Samsung Constructions built Tower 2 and was the first to complete the job although the company started a month later than rivals Hazama Corporation did on Tower 1. The price of steel being at a premium, the towers were constructed to a radical design that used cheaper super high strength reinforced concrete. In the end construction cost an estimated $1.6 billion.

Underneath the towers is Suria KLCC, a popular shopping and entertainment mall, underground parking for 4,500 cars, and the home of the Malaysian Philharmonic Orchestra—Dewan Filharmonik Petronas—a petroleum museum, a mosque, and a multimedia conference center.

MOUNT EVEREST

The tallest mountain on planet Earth from sea level to sky is Mount Everest at approximately 29,028ft (8,848m). It is rising at a rate of around 1/8-3/16 in (3-5mm) per year due to the movement of the great tectonic plates under the Himalayas. It is also edging northeastward at a rate of 1.06in (27mm) per year. The mountain range was formed relatively recently in geological time, approximately 60 million years ago.

The summit ridge of Everest lies on the border between Nepal and Tibet (currently part of China). The mountain's Nepalese name is Sagarmatha meaning "goddess of the sky," and its Tibetan name Chomolungma (or Qomolangma) means "mother goddess of the universe." Its western name is taken from Sir George Everest, the British surveyor-general of India and the first person to record the height and location of the mountain in the 1830s. The mountain was first identified as the world's highest peak in 1852 by Radhanath Sikdar, an Indian mathematician and surveyor using trigonometric calculations based on measurements made with theodolites from 150 miles (240km) away in India.

The summit was famously first reached by the New Zealand climber Edmund Hilary and the Nepalese climber Tenzing Norgay via the South Col Route in 1953. Many people have died challenging Everest, the danger not being so much the climb itself but avalanches and the dangerous and rapidly changing weather conditions. The mountain is always "booked up" for climbers and expeditions have to wait their turn; on May 10, 1993, an astonishing 40 people reached the summit. The most hazardous part of the mountain is the Khumbu Ice Fall where 19 people have died; in 1996 out of 98 people who attempted the mountain, 15 died. It is estimated that there remain about 120 corpses on the slopes.

MECCA

The holiest site in Islam is the city of Makkah al-Mukarramah, otherwise known as Mecca, in Saudi Arabia. The city is located on the sandy, narrow valley of the Wadi Ibrahim and is capital of Hejaz province. It is revered as the birthplace of Mohammed in A.D. 570. All able-bodied Muslims are required to visit Mecca at least once in their life—the pilgrimage known as the hajj—if at all possible. Non-Muslims are not permitted to enter the holy city.

The holiest place within Mecca is the al-Masjid al-Haram (the Sacred Mosque) which can hold up to 300,000 people. Inside this lies the much smaller shrine known as the Kaaba, which devotees believe was built by Abraham and contains the sacred Black Stone; and the well of Zamzam where many of the faithful like to take a spiritual drink.

Every year during the Islamic month of Dhu al-Hijjah thousands of pilgrims from around the world throng to Mecca. The observance of the hajj follows a number of rituals that are symbolic of the lives of Abraham and Hagar. Male pilgrims wear the ihram, two white unhemmed pieces of cloth and simple sandals, they do not shave or wear jewelry: this shows the equality of man and symbolizes purity and absolution from sins. The ritual starts with the Umrah or lesser Hajj, then when this is completed, pilgrims begin the *al-hajj al-akbar* or Greater Hajj that begins on the eighth day of the month.

Unfortunately in the press of people and excitement of the Hajj it is not uncommon for people to get hurt, sometime fatally. The worst incidents happen when hundreds of people attempt to get in and out through relatively narrow passageways. The worst incident happened in January 2006 when maybe as many as 350 pilgrims lost their lives.

▲
A view over the Sienne with the Eiffel Tower in the background.

Synonymous with Paris and France even though it was designed to be a temporary structure the Eiffel Tower only escaped being scrapped because it provided a good radio mast. Nevertheless, it still stands beside the River Seine on the Champ de Mars in the heart of Paris and is visible from all over the city.

When the Eiffel Tower was built for the 1889 Exposition Universelle to celebrate the centennial of the French Revolution, it was the tallest structure in the world at 1,058ft (324m) including its antenna, (986ft/300m without). 2,731 steps lead to the top of the tower—347 steps to the first level, 674 steps to the second, and 1,710 steps to the small platform at the top of the tower. The Eiffel Tower was one of the first tall buildings to contain elevators. These proved a great attraction and the ticket sales recouped almost the entire cost of the project within a year.

On a clear day, it is possible to see 42 miles (65km) in every direction from the top. Depending on the ambient temperature, the top of the tower can lean away from the sun by up to 3.25in (8cm), due to expansion of the metal on the side facing the sun. The tower was designed by and named after Gustave Eiffel, a bridge engineer. In 1887 300 workers started joining 18,038 pieces of iron and 2.5 million rivets. The tower opened on May 6 1889 and came in under budget at a cost of about $1.5 million. It was controversial from the start with many artists and elitists considering it an eyesore. At night it is lit up with thousands of light bulbs and for special occasions the Eiffel Tower changes color.

NOTRE DAME

Notre Dame de Paris (French for "Our Lady of Paris", meaning the church in Paris dedicated to Mary, the mother of Jesus), often known simply as Notre Dame in English, is a gothic cathedral on the eastern half of the Île de la Cité in Paris, France, with its main entrance to the west. While a major tourist destination, it is still used as a Roman Catholic cathedral (archbishop of Paris). The Notre Dame de Paris stands on the site of Paris' first Christian church, Saint-Étienne Basilica, which was itself built on the site of a Gallo-Roman temple to Jupiter. Notre Dame's first version was a "magnificent church" built by Childebert I, the king of the Franks in 528, and was already the cathedral of the city of Paris in the 10th century. Notre Dame de Paris is 130 m (427 ft) long. In 1160, having become the "parish church of the kings of Europe", Bishop Maurice de Sully deemed the current Parisian cathedral unworthy of its lofty role, and had it demolished shortly after he assumed the title of Bishop of Paris. According to legend, de Sully had a vision of a glorious new cathedral for Paris, and sketched it in the dirt outside of the original church. Construction began in 1163, during the reign of Louis VII, and opinion differs as to whether Bishop Maurice de Sully or Pope Alexander III laid the foundation stone of the cathedral. However, both were at the ceremony in question.

Construction of the west front, with its distinctive two towers, only began circa 1200, before the nave had been completed. Over the construction period, numerous architects worked on the site, as is evidenced by the differing styles at different heights of the west front and towers. Between 1210 and 1220, the fourth architect oversaw the construction of the level with the rose window and the great halls beneath the towers. The towers were completed around 1245, and the cathedral was completed around 1345.

PALACE OF VERSAILLES

▲

The Royal Palace gardens

The royal palace at Versailles—the Château de Versailles—was largely the creation of the Roi Soleil—the Sun King—Louis XIV. Previous monarchs had all lived in Paris but after a traumatic childhood constantly threatened by the Parisian mob and the dissident Fronde, Louis determined to live outside the confines of the city where the mob would have little chance of reaching him. Accordingly, he moved himself and the royal court to Versailles in 1682 and it became the epicenter of French power for the next hundred years or so until Louis XVI and the royal family were forced back to Paris in 1789. (Louis XVI was executed on January 21, 1793 for treason).

Versailles was initially a small hunting lodge built by Louis XIII in 1624, until Louis XIV ordered its expansion. By the time he had finished the palace was home to the royal family, the royal court, and government officers. Through the clever use of his intimidating palace Louis established himself as an absolute monarch and through his direction Versailles became a byword for opulence and excess.

Work continued on expanding Versailles even after its occupants had moved in and the palace was not complete until about 1688. The principal architect was Louis Le Vau, and the main decorator Charles Le Brun, the magnificent and extensive formal gardens were created by André Le Nôtre. In fact Louis poached them from his finance minister Nicolas Fouquet who had used them at his own extravagant chateau, Vaux-le-Vicomte.

Louis' XV and XVI extended Versailles with the addition of the Grand Trianon, the Petit Trianon, and the Petit Hameau, for Marie Antoinette. During the French Revolution Versailles was pillaged of most of it rich and valuable furnishings. In time Versailles was restored and became a museum.

MILLAU VIADUCT

The Millau Viaduct consists of an eight-span steel roadway supported by seven concrete piers. The roadway weighs 36,000 tonnes and is 2,460 m long, measuring 32 m wide by 4.2 m deep. The six central spans each measure 342 m with the two outer spans measuring 204 m. The roadway has a slope of 3% descending from south to north, and curves in plan section on a 20 km radius to give drivers better visibility. It carries two lanes of traffic in each direction.

The piers range in height from 77–246 m, and taper in their longitudinal section from 24.5 m at the base to 11 m at the deck. Each pier is composed of 16 framework sections, each section weighing 2,230 tonnes. These sections were assembled on site from pieces of 60 tonnes, 4 m wide and 17 m long, made in factories in Lauterbourg and Fos-sur-Mer by Eiffage. The piers each support 97 m tall pylons. The piers were assembled first, together with some temporary supports, before the decks were slid out across the piers by satellite-guided hydraulic rams that moved the deck 600 mm every 4 minutes.

The viaduct is the tallest vehicular bridge in the world, nearly twice as tall as the previous tallest vehicular bridge in Europe, the Europabrücke in Austria. (The proposed Strait of Messina Bridge in Italy, if constructed, would be taller.)

The Millau Viaduct is the second highest vehicular bridge measured from the roadway elevation. Its deck, at approximately 270 m above the Tarn, is slightly higher than the New River Gorge Bridge in West Virginia in the United States, which is 267 m above the New River. The Royal Gorge Bridge in Colorado, United States has a deck considerably higher than either, at 321 m above the Arkansas River. Construction began on 10 October 2001 and was intended to take three years, but weather conditions put work on the bridge behind schedule. A revised schedule aimed for the bridge to be opened in January 2005. The viaduct was officially inaugurated by President Chirac on 14 December 2004 to open for traffic on 16 December, several weeks ahead of the revised schedule. The construction of the bridge is depicted in a documentary of the Discovery Channel 'Megastructures' series.

The ultimate fairy tale castle was built between 1869 and 1892 by King Ludwig II of Bavaria on the old ruins of two small castles, Vorder and Hinterhohenschwangau, overlooking Pöllat gorge in Bavaria. Heavily influenced by his friend the composer Richard Wagner the design of the castle was a complete fantasy that drew heavily on the imagery of the Germanic myths of *Lohengrin* and *Tannhäuser*. Ludwig did not live to see it completed and only spent 11 nights there in spring 1884.

As a child Ludwig had been fascinated by swans and especially the legend of the swan knight Lohengrin. It was also the heraldic beast of the Counts of Schwangau, who Ludwig considered his ancestors. Accordingly, the image of a swan appears all around the castle.

The architect commissioned to created Ludwig's "fantasy in stone" was Christian Jank, a stage designer by profession. Neuschwanstein was designed in 13th century Late Romanesque Germanic style out of brick faced with limestone blocks, but incorporating all the most modern amenities, including a central heating system for the entire building, running water on all floors, automatic flush toilets, a hot water system for the kitchen and bathrooms, a modern kitchen with automatic spits and cupboards heated with hot air, and a winter garden (in homage to Tannhäuser) accessed by a huge glass sliding door.

When Ludwig died work initially stopped until a simplified version of the original plan was finished in 1891. The castle was opened to the public seven weeks after Ludwig's death and has attracted thousands of visitors ever since. Ludwig built three extraordinary castles, Neuschwanstein, Linderhof, and Herrenchiemsee, plus plans for a fourth. In his lifetime the castle was called New Hohenschwangau Castle, this was changed after his death to Neuschwanstein, meaning New Swan Castle.

The 512ft (150m) high flat topped rock in the center of Athens is known as the Acropolis, which mean "high city" in Greek. Its other name is Cecropia after the the legendary serpent-man, Kekrops or Cecrops, the first Athenian king. This elevated site has been occupied from Neolithic times and was in continual use as a residential area and cult place, particularly for Athena, the patron goddess of Athens. Most of the temples and ruins we see today date from the classical period of Ancient Greece during the Golden Age of Perikles.

The principal buildings on the Acropolis are the monumental gateway known as the Propylaea, and to its right the small temple to Athene Nike. The Erechtheum is dedicated to Athena Polias and is remarkable for its caryatids—columns in the shape of goddesses.

The most famous building however is the magnificent ruin of the Parthenon or Temple of Athena Parthenos. This was built in the Doric order between 447 and 438 B.C. and was designed by the architects Iktinos and Kallikrates, with sculptures by Pheidias. Its has 17 columns down its long sides and eight columns at either end, in the center in an area known as the cella, once stood the huge chryselephantine cult statue of Athena, made by Pheidias. The entire temple is optically adjusted so that it appears absolutely symmetrical. Over its history the Parthenon has been a temple, a Byzantine church, a Latin church and a Muslim mosque.

Until 1867 the Parthenon had remained in remarkably good condition but when the Turks conquered Athens they stored their gunpowder in the Parthenon. Fatally, during the Venetian seige led by Admiral Morosini a Venetian bomb fell on the ancient temple and the resulting explosion blew off the roof and left the Parthenon in ruins.

The largest public games in the entire Roman empire were held at the Amphitheatrum Flavium, better known as simply the Colosseum. In antiquity this was the scene of some of the bloodiest public spectacles ever as thousands of animals and people met a gruesome end in front of cheering crowds, all in the name of entertainment.

In 72 A.D, just a few years after the great fire of Rome in 64 A.D., Emperor Vespasian ordered the construction of a new ampitheater over the site of Nero's lake and below the Domus Aurea, his extensive palace, which had been built across the slope of the Palatine. The ampitheater was not completed for another eight years by which time his son Titus was emperor. The Roman historian Dio Cassius recorded that 10,000 wild animals were killed in the first hundred days of celebration which inaugurated the opening. Later still Emperor Domitian ordered improvements and the top extension.

Roughly elliptical in shape so that the audience was as close to the action as possible, the Colosseum could hold between 50,000 and 75,000 spectators. It is made up of three floors of arcades and a fourth storey with windows. Below ground under a moveable floor containing numerous trapdoors, were the holding pits and cages for animal and gladiators. On occasion the arena could be flooded for maritime reenactments.

When the Roman Empire collapsed and extravagant public entertainments stopped the Colosseum was abandoned: for a time it was used by medieval clans as their city fortress but it was constantly being plundered for stone building materials until in 1749 Pope Benedict XIV declared it a holy site on account of the numbers of Christian martyrs who had died there and forbade the desecration of the building. This action undoubtedly saved the Colosseum from diasppearing altogether.

LEANING TOWER OF PISA

La Torre di Pisa was not intended to be a leaning tower at all but rather a beautiful and upright campanile or bell tower in the Campo dei Miracoli (Field of Miracles) adjacent to the cathedral in Pisa, Italy. It was built as a sign of Pisa's importance and wealth and was completed intermittently over three stages over a period of some 200 years.

Work on constructing the tower started on August 9, 1173 but only on a 10ft (3m) foundation. The first stage comprising a white marble campanile is made up of blind arches and pillars topped with classical capitals. The second and third levels were started in 1178 at which point the tower developed a perceptible tilt. Construction halted in 1180 because Pisa was involved in continuous expensive conflicts with Genoa, Lucca, and Florence. In fact this enforced delay saved the tower from collapse as it gave the subsoil time to settle.

Construction resumed in 1272 and another four floors were added but at an angle to compensate for the tilt, work stopped again in 1284 when Pisa was defeated by the Genoa at the Battle of Meloria. Almost a hundred years later—1372—work restarted on the bell chamber and the bells were hung. The final, largest, and seventh bell (one for each note of the musical scale) was eventually put in place in 1655. Many attempts were made to correct the lean. Most notably in 1838 when the base of the tower was dug out of the subsoil, but the tower flooded and the angle of lean increased. During the 1930s Beneto Mussolini ordered that the tower be made vertical but the effort only resulted in the tower sinking further. In recent years with international help and advice, the tower has at last been stabilized.

The tiny sovereign state and smallest independent nation in the world is the Vatican City, a landlocked enclave within the city of Rome. In is governed by the Pope in his position as the Bishop of Rome and totals only 108.7acres (44 hectares). The Vatican is named for the Mons Vaticanus or Vatican Hill, a part of Rome that pre-dates Christianity and is separated from the rest of Rome by the River Tiber. St. Peter's Basilica, the Apostolic Palace with its Sistine Chapel, and various other buildings were built on the adjacent Vatican Fields.

Work started on St Peter's at the beginning of the 16th century by the direction of Pope Nicolas V, when he died Julius II took over and in 1547 the sculptor Michaelangelo Buonarotti was appointed architect. He revised the design with the inclusion of the magnificent dome. St Peter's was finished in 1626 two years after Michaelangelo's death, it is the largest church in the world.

Another of Michaelangelo's works decorates the ceiling of the Sistine Chapel, in the Apostolic Palace. The chapel is the same size as the Old Testament gives for the Temple of Solomon (134ft by 44ft/40.93m by 13.41m). It was built beween 1473 and 1484 on the orders of Pope Sixtus IV. The main ceiling is a flattened barrel vault and this is the location of one of the most famous paintings in the world. In 1508 Pope Julius II commissioned Michaelangelo to paint the Sistine Chapel ceiling: he changed the Pope's ideas and took on the fresco work entirely by himself after he fell out with his assistants. It was an enormous undertaking, 30ft (9m) up in the air and one which by his own account Michaelangelo hated, but his burining ambition drove him to complete the project. It took 20 months of hard toil.

▲
A Statue of St. Peter

▶
Detail of St. Peters cathedral

IN HONOREM PRINCIPIS APOST PAVLVS V BVRGHESIVS ROMANVS PONT MAX AN MDCXII PONT VII

▲ *The Rialto bridge* ▶ *San Marco square*

▲ *Some Gondalas resting*

The Italian city of Venice is universally agreed to be one of the most beautiful cities in the world. Called the "city of canals" it is built on ancient wooden piles in the marshy Venetian Lagoon on the northeast Adriatic coast. The first settlers were refugees fleeing from the invading Lombards in 568 who settled in the safety of the marshes of the Po estuary. There they started to build their city amongst the numerous islands of the salt water lagoon.

Gradually Venice grew in importance and became a prosperous city state ruled by an elected Doge. Wealth came thanks to Venice's strategic location as a trading center between East and West, particularly for the spice trade, with her merchants taking a cut of the profits both ways. The city became an independent republic with a maritime empire that was a force to be reckoned with having control of the Adriatic, much of the Aegean (including Cyprus and Crete), and a muscular presence in the Mediterranean.

Venice became an imperial power in the wake of the Fourth Crusade, that took Constantinople in 1204 and established the Latin Empire which lasted until 1453. A great deal of booty was taken back to Venice, including the Winged Lion of St. Mark which became the city's symbol. During the Renaissance Venetian art, architecture, and literature influenced the world.

The wealth acquired by her merchants and traders was poured into the city and some of the most beautiful buildings anywhere were built. The Republic lasted until Napoleon Bonaparte conquered Venice on May 12, 1797 after which it declined in commerce and prosperity. After years of changing hands politically Venice became part of Italy in 1866.

▲ *Venice from Campanile*

PALACE OF THE PARLIAMENT

▲

A view from a balcony of the Palace

The Palatul Parlamentului or Palace of the Parliament in Bucharest, Romania, is one of the largest buildings in the world. Universally known by its old name of Casa Poporului, it was built during the last days Nicolae Ceausescu in an amalgamation of various architectural styles. To build such a vast complex about a fifth of old Bucharest, including homes and churches was destroyed. The building is 886ft (270m) long and 12 stories high (282ft–86m), plus 302ft (92m) of four basement levels. The building is still incomplete as work halted when the Ceausescu regime fell in 1989.

Inside the Casa Poporului there are 1,100 rooms many of them full of marble with no extravagance was spared and everything was sourced from Romania. It is said that so much marble was required that tombstones across Romania had to be made from other materials. The numbers are staggering—some 480 crystal chandeliers—the biggest weighs 3tons (2.7mt) and uses over 7,000 bulbs—hundreds of mirrors and lights adorn the ceilings and shine across thousands of tons of steel and bronze on the monumental doors and ornamentation. Luxury fabrics such as velvet and brocade swathe the windows and in the principal chambers elaborate gold and silver passementerie and embroideries adorn the curtains. Walnut, oak, sweet cherry, elm, sycamore, and maple were used in abundance for parquet floors and wainscotting, plus vast swathes of carpet. Carpet weaving machines were moved into the building to make the 14 ton carpet for the hall. The Sala Unirii (Unification Hall) even has a sliding ceiling designed to be wide enough for a helicopter.

The building was originally intended to house all the organs of the Communist state, today it is the home of the Romanian parliament, museums, and a conference centerbut most of the building is unused.

HERMITAGE

▲ *The Winter palace by Neva*   ▶ *The main entrance to Winter Palace*

The Hermitage Museum in St. Petersburg, Russia is one of the largest and oldest art galleries and museums in the world. The collections are displayed in six buildings, the most impressive of which, the Winter Palace, used to be the official residence of the Russian czars. The collection was started by Catherine the Great in 1764 when she ordered her foreign ambassadors to purchase the best European paintings available. The result was some 250 paintings from great collections in France, Saxony, and England. She called her private art gallery "my hermitage" and allowed few people to see it. Catherine's predecessors expanded and improved the collections. The New Hermitage was commissioned by Czar Nicholas I from the neoclassicist German architect Leo von Klenze for his growing collection of ancient Greek, Roman, and Egyptian antiquities. This was the first purpose-built art gallery in Eastern Europe, and opened to the public in 1852.

Following the October Revolution the Hermitage collections became public property and were further increased when private art collections were nationalized and incorporated into the museum. At the end of World War II in 1945 the the Red Army occupied Berlin and looted many artworks including much of Heinrich Schliemann's ancient gold treasures from Troy and many important paintings.

On Stalin's orders a number of precious Hermitage pictures were sold including Raphael's *Madonna Alba*, Titian's *Venus with a Mirror* and Jan van Eyck's *Annunciation*. Most went to form the basis of the National Gallery of Art in Washington, D.C.

The vast Hermitage collections include the Russian imperial regalia, Faberge jewelery, and hoards of ancient gold from Eastern Europe and Western Asia. The collection of Western art includes works by Michelangelo, da Vinci, Rubens, Van Dyck, Rembrandt, Lorraine, Watteau, Canaletto, Canova, Rodin, Monet, Pissarro, Renoir, Cezanne, Van Gogh, Gauguin, Picasso, and Matisse.

RED SQUARE

▲

St. Basil Cathedral

▲ *The Annunciation cathedral (left) and the Assumption cathedral (right)*

▶ *St. Basil Cathedral at night from Red Square*

All roads in Russia lead to Red Square, or so it seems. This vast plaza gets its name from the Russian word krasnaya which means red or beautiful, the latter which was originally applied to St Basil's Cathedral and then moved to mean the square. The original land was covered with wooden buildings until Czar Ivan III's 1493 edict to remove all potential fire hazards. At this time it acquired the name Pozhar meaning "burnt out place" and started to be used as a convenient market place and soon became the primary market in Moscow. As time went on it was also used for important public ceremonies and proclamations, and even occasionally as the coronation venue for Russia's czars. This usage grew and the square continued to grow in importance until it was used for official ceremonies by all Russian governments since it was established.

The name Red Square probably replaced Pozhar sometime during the 17th century. In Soviet times the square became familiar around the world through television reports as the site of the great shows of military might for the May Day Parade in front of the Soviet government hierarchy standing on top of Lenin's Mausoleum. The square separates the Kremlin, the former royal citadel and currently the official residence of the President of Russia, from the historic merchant quarter, known as Kitay-gorod. Magnificent St Basil's Cathedral occupies one side of the square, its proper name means "Cathedral of the Intercession" and named in homage to the prophet who forewarned of the 1547 Moscow fire. St Basil's was built in the 1550s to celebrate the capture by Ivan IV (aka Ivan the Terrible) of the Mongol stronghold of Kazan.

In 1991, the Red Square was added to UNESCO's list of World Heritage Sites.

ALHAMBRA

The Moorish rulers of southern Spain built a combined palace and fortress across a hilly terrace on the south-eastern border of the city of Granada. Called the Alhambra or Red Castle it is named for walls of red sun-dried bricks—*tapia*—which are made of fine gravel and clay. It is famous for the beauty of its Moorish gardens and elegantly elaborate buildings and interiors. The palace is surrounded by a strongly fortified wall, which is strengthened by thirteen towers.

The principal parts of the palace date from its main building phase which started during the reign of Mahomet Ibn Al Ahmar in 1248 and continued under his succesors until 1354. Granada was conquered by Christians in 1492 when the Moors were expelled to return to North Africa. The Christians vandalized much of the palace by destroying its delicate carvings and artworks and looting its valuables. The Alhambra was "improved" by modernisers over the centuries, Charles V (1516–1556) had altered the layout and rebuilt parts in the Renaissance style, in the early 18th century Philip V (1700–1746) Italianised the rooms and built in effect a new palace in the heart of the old Moorish building.

In 1812 some of the towers were blown up by the French under Count Sebastiani then Napoleon ordered that the entire complex be blown up. Luckily a crippled French soldier defused the explosives and so saved the Alhambra for posterity. As if that were not enough, an earthquake in 1821 caused further damage.

Restoration of the Alhambra finally started in 1828 by the architect Jose Contreras, two years later Ferdinand VII helped financially. Contreras's work was continued after his death by his son Rafael and then in turn by his grandson Mariano.

SAGRADA FAMILIA

The highlight of the Catalan city of Barcelona is the extraordinary La Sagrada Família (in Catalan) or La Sagrada Familia (in Spanish) basilica. It is the most popular tourist attraction in Spain even though still in the process of being built, it is optimistically hoped to be complete around 2026 for the 100th anniversary of Gaudi's death.

The basilica was planned in the late 19th century and work started in the 1880s under the supervision of architect Francesco del Villar. He soon quarreled with the founding association and the job was handed to the maverick Catalan architect Antoni Gaudí in 1883. Gaudí scrapped the original design and started again, it was the start of a 40-year project for him and is his most extraordinary work. He devoted his last 15 years exclusively to Sagrada Familia until his death in 1926. Work was interrupted by the Spanish Civil War in 1935 when parts of the unfinished building along with Gaudí's models and workshop were destroyed by anarchists.

Work recommenced in the 1950s based on reconstructions of Gaudí's lost plans as well as on modern adaptations. The main part of the nave was completed in 2005, and work then turned to the supporting structure for the main tower of Jesus Christ. The basilica (it is not a cathedral) is rich with Christian symbolism as Gaudí intended. It is most notable for its 18 spindle-shaped towers which represent, in descending order of height: Jesus Christ (surmounted eventually with a giant cross), the Virgin Mary, the four Evangelists—their towers will sport their symbols, a a bull for St. Luke, an angel for St. Matthew, an eagle for St. John, and a lion for St. Mark—and the 12 Apostles.

▲
Interior ceiling of the La Sagrada Familia

▼
Barcelona from the roof of the La Sagrada Familia

▲
The impressive front door to the cathedral

EPHESUS

▲
The Celcis Library ruins

▲
Old Roman Amphitheater at Ephesus

▶
Statue of Arete between two marble columns at the Celcus Library

One of the greatest cities of the Ionian Greeks in Asia Minor was Ephesus, located in Lydia where the Cayster river flows into the Aegean Sea. Then later, during the Roman Empire, Ephesus grew even more important as the capital of proconsular Asia, which covered the western part of Asia Minor and bore the title of "the first and greatest metropolis of Asia." Reasons for this claim were the magnificent Temple of Artemis, the largest building of the ancient world, according to Pausanias, and one of the Seven Wonders of the World, sadly almost nothing remains of the temple today. Mycenaean pottery has been found in excavations around Ephesus including the many-breasted "Lady of Ephesus."

Other ancient sites include the Roman era Celsus Library, and the huge Roman ampitheater, which could hold 25,000 spectators. The population of Ephasus in 100 A.D. is estimated to have been anything up to 500,000 inhabitants, making it largest city in Roman Asia and one of the largest cities anywhere. In addition the Romans built several major bath complexes, and one of the most advanced aqueduct systems in the ancient world with multiple aqueducts of various sizes to supply different areas of the city.

Ephesus became an important center for early Christianity after St Paul used the city as a base. He became embroiled in a dispute with artisans, whose livelihood depended on the Temple of Artemis there and wrote 1 Corinthians from Ephesus. Later St Paul wrote to the Christian community at Ephesus.

The Roman city of Ephesus was abandoned in the sixth century AD when the harbor despite considerable efforts to dredge it, completely filled up with river silt preventing access to the Aegean Sea.

▲
Greek columns at Hadrian's library

HAGIA SOPHIA

The Virgin, Byzantine mosaic in the interior of Hagia Sophia

This former Eastern Orthodox church, then mosque, and now Ayasofya Museum lies in the center of Istambul, Turkey. However the basilica is still best known as Hagia Sophia— Church of Holy Wisdom— and is one of the most ambitious ancient monuments built since the fall of Rome. Its loss to the Ottoman Turks following the fall of Constantinople in 1453 is considered by the Greek Orthodox faithful to be one of the great tragedies of Christendom.

Hagia Sophia was built under the personal supervision of emperor Justinian I and dedicated on December 27, 537. It is one of the greatest surviving examples of Byzantine architecture with its magnificent decorated interior rich with green and white polychrome marbles, purple porphyry, gold mosaics, and marble columns. On the exterior, simple stuccoed walls show off the huge array of massed vaults and domes.

Hagia Sophia was the largest cathedral anywhere for 1,000 years until the completion of the cathedral in Seville, and even today it remains the fourth largest in size (not height) in the world. The basilica is remarkable for its central dome 184ft (56m) high, with a diameter of 102ft (31m) which transforms itself from a hemisphere at the top to a square below as it distributes the colossal weight of the dome downwards so that it apparently floats on four great arches. In addition an unbroken arcade of 40 windows pierce the base of the dome producing a mystical quality of light around the interior.

Inevitably in such an earthquake prone area, Hagia Sophia has suffered: the dome collapsed after an earthquake in 558 and its replacement fell in 563. Partial collapses in 989 and for some years after, necessitated running repairs. In 1346 under Süleyman the Magnificent, extra pieces were attached to prevent further collapses.

Hagia Sofia interior

EDEN PROJECT

Built in a disused china clay quarry near St Austell in Cornwall, England is an ongoing environmental project that explores the relationship between people and plants. Called the Eden Project it opened to the public in March 2001 and features two huge transparent biomes that each emulate a natural environment and contain the relevant plant species that grow there. The first dome contains a tropical environment and is filled with exotic plants found in the jungles and rainforests of the world. The second dome has warm temperate, Mediterranean-type environment and features the plants that grow in such conditions.

An important aspect of the Eden Project is a serious ongoing environmental and educational study, which aims to safeguard the Earth and prevent mankind from destroying the many benefits provided by nature by showcasing the crucial interdependence of plants and people. All the various kinds of known medicinal uses for the plants are listed beside each plant and many educational displays explain and elucidate the purpose of the various plants: these are intended to be both fun and educational.

The Eden Centre has proved to be a major tourist attraction and is continually developing its scope and ambition. This is an extremely environmentally aware project and strongly features the problem of Global Warming and what mankind can do about it. The Eden Project recycles as much as possible, with all litter areas split into five or more compartments for plastic, food, paper, and other general waste, which is all recycled. The massive amounts of water required to create the humid conditions of the Tropical Biome, as well as to serve the toilet facilities, are all sanitized rain water that would otherwise collect at the bottom of the quarry.

HOUSES OF PARLIAMENT

▲
The Houses of Parliament from the River Thames

The Palace of Westminster is called the "Mother of Parliaments" and sits beside the north bank of the River Thames in London, England. Also known as the Houses of Parliament this distinctive Victorian Gothic building is the seat of government for the United Kingdom.

The site—originally called Thorney Island—has been occupied since before the arrival of the Saxons. Canute the Great (reigned 1016 to 1035) was probably the first to use a building there as a royal residence but Edward the Confessor was the first to build a royal palace here at about the same time as he built Westminster Abbey, around 1045–1050.

After the Norman Conquest in 1066, King William I made his base at the Tower of London, but later moved his court to the Palace of Westminster which remained the monarch's principal residence throughout the late medieval period. The oldest existing parts of the Palace, Westminster Hall and the Great Hall, date from the reign William II. In 1295 The Model Parliament, the first official Parliament of England, met in the Palace and since then, almost all Parliaments have met in the Palace.

Westminster remained the monarch's chief London residence until fire destroyed parts of the building in 1529. So in 1530, King Henry VIII took York Palace from Cardinal Wolsey, renamed it the Palace of Whitehall, and used it as his principal residence. Much of the palace was destroyed by a catastrophic fire in 1834 and the present buildings date from the rebuild. Two principal architects worked on the project, Sir Charles Barry and Augustus Welby Pugin, to produce one of the very best examples of Gothic revival architecture.

Perhaps the most famous feature of the Houses of Parliament is the Clock Tower which holds the massive bronze bell known as Big Ben.

▲
The London Eye (left) with the Houses of Parliament (right)

STONEHENGE

One of the most famous prehistoric sites in the world is the Neolithic and Bronze Age megalithic monument known as Stonehenge, found in Wiltshire, England. The complex includes a landscape of earthworks that surround a circular setting of large standing stones which archaeologists estimate were erected between 2500 BC and 2000 B.C., although the surrounding circular earth bank and ditch—the earliest phase of the monument—have been dated to about 3100 BC.

Archaeologists and engineers are uncertain as to how exactly Stonehenge was built and how the stones were transported to the site in a period well before any form of mechanization. Also, the prehistoric reason for and use of the stone circle is widely disputed. Some experts think that it was a stone copy of more common timber structures that dotted Salisbury Plain at the time, such as those that stood at Durrington Walls. Possibly timber was associated by prehistoric peoples with the living, while stone was associated with the ancestral dead. They posit that Stonehenge could have been the terminus of a long, ritualised funerary procession route for the dead, which began during sunrise in the east at Woodhenge and Durrington Walls, and moved down the Avon river and then along the Avenue to reach Stonehenge in the west by sunset. This journey from wood to stone via water was a symbolic journey from life to death. This provides a ritual role for Stonehenge that takes into account its numerous burials and its presence within a wider landscape of sacred sites.

The site and its surroundings were added to the UNESCO's list of World Heritage Sites in 1986 in a co-listing with Avebury henge monument. Stonehenge is owned and managed by English Heritage while the surrounding downland is owned by the National Trust.

TOWER BRIDGE

Victorian London was a thriving city at the heart of a world wide empire which was growing in wealth and importance. The city likewise was experiencing phenominal growth especially in the dockland area of East London. This increased commerce necessitated a new bridge across the River Thames downstream of London Bridge; the problem was that a traditional fixed bridge would cut off access to the port facilities in the Pool of London between London Bridge and the Tower of London. Accordingly, in 1876, a public competition was announced to find a solution to the problem. Of over 50 designs submitted the winning entry was from Horace Jones who produced a design for a medieval looking, two tower, bascule bridge which could be raised in the central span to allow river traffic to pass. The bascules would be raised by a hydraulic mechanism powered by pressurised water stored in six accumulators and pumped by steam engines, these would raise and lower the movable roadways in under two minutes. The towers themselves would rise 200ft (61m) above the Thames and be joined by a glass-covered walkway for pedestrians. Construction started in 1886 and took eight years. Five major contractors were used and 432 construction workers. Jones died in 1887 leaving his chief engineer, Sir John Wolfe-Barry to oversee the project. The latter changed the original plans to produce the much more ornate Victorian gothic structure that we see today. The bridge was opened on June 30, 1894 by the Prince of Wales and his wife Alexandra of Denmark. The public were not at all enamoured of the bridge initially, generally thinking it hideous.

When the bridge opened to river traffic in 1894, it was raised and lowered 1,000 times per year.

The Niagara River on the border between the United States and Canada flows across a massive heavily eroded rock lip to create the Niagara Falls, one of the great natural features of North America. This popular tourist site is shared between the twin cities of Niagara Falls, New York and Niagara Falls, Ontario.

The falls are actually three separate waterfalls: the Horseshoe Falls (or Canadian Falls) and the smaller, adjacent Bridal Veil Falls, both of which drop around 170ft (52m), and the American Falls that drop 70ft (21m). The Horseshoe Falls are about 2,600ft (792m) wide, while the American Falls are 1,060ft (323m) wide. Over 6 million cubic feet (168,000cu m) of water tumble over the long crestline every minute, making Niagara the most powerful waterfall in North America.

The historical origin of Niagara Falls goes back 10,000 years to the Wisconsin glaciation which also created the Great Lakes. This last great continental ice sheet engulfed the entire eastern side of North America grinding up and moving rocks and soil, and in the process deepening river channels to make lakes. Other channels became dammed with debris, forcing the rivers into new channels. As the ice melted back northwards the meltwater drained to the lowest land point from the upper Great Lakes to become the Niagara River.

Over time the water cut a gorge across the Niagara Escarpment, exposing ancient marine rocks and three major formations. The erosion process continues and, despite being slowed by engineering, they will eventually recede far enough to drain most of Lake Erie, because its base is higher than the bottom of the falls.

One of the most famous and exclusive golf clubs in the world is Augusta National Golf Club, the site of the annual Masters Tournament when the spotlight of the golfing world turns on Georgia. In theory anyone can become a member of Augusta National Golf Club but as it carries a limited roll of some 300 members the opportunities are few and far between. Membership is by invitation only and aspiring members can only hope to be invited, no matter how wealthy they are; the fees are rumored to be between $25,000 and $50,000. Women are allowed to play the course as guests of a member but no woman has ever been invited to join the club. The controversy that was aroused by such stringent membership rules led the Club to voluntarily allow the tv broadcasts of the 2003 and 2004 Masters Tournaments to be transmitted without commercials.

The highly desirable green jacket with club logo on the left breast is worn only by members of the Augusta National. It was the inspiration of club co-founder Clifford Roberts, who wanted visiting patrons to be able to identify each other easily. The winner of each year's Masters Tournament becomes an honorary member and is accordingly awarded a green jacket presented by the outgoing winner.

The course at Augusta was designed by Bobby Jones and is considered to be his best piece of work. Virtually every golf course in the U.S. has a rating but almost uniquely Augusta National has never been rated. However, unofficially during the 1990 Masters Tournament, a team of USGA raters organized by Golf Digest evaluated the course and gave it an unofficial rating of 76.2 and a slope of 148.

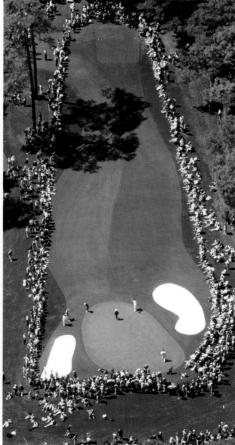

CAPE CANAVAREL

▲ *Aerial view showing the Delta II launch pads at Complex 17 on Cape Canaveral Air Force Station.*

▶ *The STS-36 vehicle and launch platform rolling out to Launch Pad 39A*

Next to the Atlantic coast in Brevard County, Florida, sits a strip of land called Cape Canaveral (or Cabo Cañaveral in Spanish) The site is world famous as the location of the Kennedy Space Center, and the Cape Canaveral Air Force Station from where the United States launch most of their spacecraft; all manned U.S. spaceflights have launched from Cape Canaveral. The name Cañaveral was given to the area by the first Spanish explorers, and it literally means "canebrake" and can be interpreted as "Cape of Canes."

Cape Canaveral was chosen for rocket launches to take advantage of the Earth's rotation and make the most of centrifugal force (at maximum at the equator). Rockets need to be launched eastward to take advantage of the rotation. It is also necessary to have the downrange area as empty as possible in case of accidents—so hense the use of this, the most south-easterly location on mainland U.S.A. The first rocket launch from the Cape was Bumper 8 from Launch Pad 3 on July 24, 1950. On February 6, 1959 the first successful test firing of a Titan intercontinental ballistic missile was accomplished here.

Between 1963 to 1973 Cape Canaveral was called Cape Kennedy in tribute to President John F. Kennedy who had been a cheerleader for the space program. After his assassination in 1963, his widow Jacqueline Kennedy suggested to President Lyndon Johnson that renaming the space facility would be an appropriate memorial. Johnson agreed but recommended the renaming not just of the facility, but of the entire cape. The name change was officially approved in 1964, but was unpopular in Florida and in 1973 the state passed a law restoring the former 400-year-old name, but the space center retains the name Kennedy.

▼ *Liftoff of the Atlas V rocket from Complex 41*

WALT DISNEY WORLD

▲

Expedition Everest at Disney's Animal Kingdom

▼

Against the fairytale backdrop of Cinderella Castle in the Magic Kingdom are Mickey and Minnie Mouse

▲

One of Disney's newest stars, Chicken Little

▼

Kali River Rapids in the Animal Kingdom

▲

Big Thunder mountain railroad

▶

Cinderella Castle in the Magic Kingdom

The Walt Disney World Resort comprises the largest and most popular collection of theme parks in the world—Magic Kingdom, Epcot, Disney-MGM Studios, and Disney's Animal Kingdom—all located just south of the city of Orlando at Lake Buena Vista and Bay Lake in Orange Country and Osceola County, Florida. When Walt Disney died in 1966 plans for "the Florida Project" were well under way and construction was able to start a year later on Walt Disney World. It was designed to be bigger and better than the original Disneyland in California and included the construction of hotels and other facilities so that people could stay at the resort. The Magic Kingdom opened to the public on October 1, 1971 and covers an area of 107 acres (43 ha) in Bay Lake. Its highlight is Main Street USA with its fairytale Cinderella Castle. The second Florida theme park, Epcot Center—"Experimental Prototype Community of Tomorrow"—was Walt Disney's pet project although the finished park differed greatly from his original concept by the time it opened to the public on October 1, 1982. It is dedicated to international culture and technological innovation and covers over 300 acres (121ha). The third theme park is Disney-MGM Studios dedicated to Hollywood classic movies and popular tv entertainment. It opened on May 1, 1989 and covers some 135 acres (55ha). The fourth park is Disney's Animal Kingdom which opened on April 22, 1998 and is themed around live animals and extinct dinosaurs in an area of more than 500 acres (202ha). The resort is continually expanding and improving, it also includes two water parks (Typhoon Lagoon and Blizzard Beach), a sports complex, an auto race track, and six golf courses. There are 20 hotels and hundreds of shops and restaurants. Walt Disney World employs over 53,000 people to look after it's millions of visitors each year.

▲

Kilmanjaro Safari in Disney's Animal Kingdom

GOLDEN GATE BRIDGE

The Golden Gate Bridge was declared by the American Society of Civil Engineers to be one of the Modern Wonders of the World. It designed by Joseph Strauss, already successful bridge engineer, to span the Golden Gate Strait which joins the Pacific Ocean to San Francisco Bay. After long years of consultation and fund raising, construction started on January 5, 1933 and was completed in April 1947 at a cost of $35 million to link Marin County headland to the San Francisco Peninsula and the city of San Francisco.

During the construction program about 30 workers fell off the bridge, normally all would have died but the bridge had an innovative safety net which saved some 19 men: they formed themselves into the *Halfway to Hell Club*. When the Golden Gate Bridge was opened to traffic at midday on May 28, 1937 it was the longest suspension bridge in the world, a title it kept until 1964. Standing 220ft (67m) above high water, the bridge carries six lanes of traffic with walkways on either side for 1.7 miles (2.7km) and is designated U.S. Route 101 and California State Route 1. The two towers are 4,200ft (1,280m) apart and rise 746ft (230m).

The bridge is painted International Orange, a color specially chosen to enhance its beauty and compliment its spectacular surroundings. In addition the color makes the bridge easier to see during the frequent San Francisco fogs. A total of 38 painters are kept busy keeping the paintwork up to scratch. The bridge is a regular and popular backdrop for many Hollywood movies and television dramas, making it an instantly recognizable location for people all over the world.

GRAND CANYON

The largest and most awe inspiring natural feature in North America is the Grand Canyon in northern Arizona. President Theodore Roosevelt was a great champion of the canyon and did much to protect its future, including helping the creation of the Grand Canyon National Park, which was one of the first national parks in the U.S. and in which most of the canyon resides. The exposed layers of sediment (many of which were formed under the sea) and rocks reveal almost two billion years of Earth's geological history.

Native Americans have lived in settlements cut into the canyons since before recorded history; while the first westerner to see the Grand Canyon was García López de Cárdenas from Spain in 1540.

The Grand Canyon is part of the Colorado River basin and was created through erosion and water action in recent geological times. The Grand Canyon itself is probably less than five or six million years old with the deepest features cut within the last two million years. The deep canyons were created by the fast running waters of the Colorado River cutting down through the soft rock strata at the same time as the Colorado Plateau was being thrust upwards—starting about 65 million years ago—by deep underground seismic action.

Exactly how and why the features were formed is still the subject of heated debate among experts, but some facts are known: 5.3 million years ago the base level and the course of the Colorado River changed when the Gulf of California opened, this drained the Colorado quicker and increased the rate of erosion cutting the deepest canyon walls.

▲
The Colorado river cuts through the canyon

HOOVER DAM

On the border between Arizona and Nevada lies the vast curved edifice of Hoover Dam which halts the course of the Colorado River in the Black Canyon. It was built in 1931 during the height of the Great Depression and provided much needed work for eight thousand people. The dam was originally intended to be built in Boulder Canyon and the name stuck during construction, even though the location changed. Before building could start in 1930 the Colorado River had to be diverted by blasting massive tunnels through the canyon walls. At the official beginning of the project on September 17, 1930 it was announced that the new dam would be named Hoover Dam in line with convention honoring the sitting President. At the same time and at the height of the Depression, Hoover was campaigning for reelection and keen to take credit for creating jobs; a Congressional Act of February 14, 1931, made the name "Hoover Dam" official.

When Hoover lost the presidential election to Franklin Roosevelt in 1932, the former's name was removed from the project and it reverted to being Boulder Dam. However under President Truman in 1947 the name was officially changed back to Hoover Dam because Herbert Hoover had been crucial to its construction, first as Secretary of Commerce and then later as President.

The dam was completed in under five years in 1936, (two years ahead of schedule) and under budget at $165 million. The dam is 726ft (221m) high and 660ft (201m) thick at the base. Interestingly the only reason that the dam is curved is so that people feel safer, in fact it is so strong and thick that this feature is unnecessary. Behind the dam sits Lake Mead, the reservoir named for Elwood Mead, who oversaw the construction of the dam.

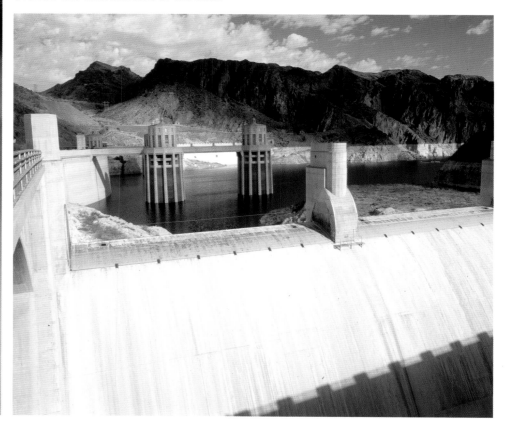

INDIANAPOLIS MOTOR SPEEDWAY

Pole sitter Elliott Sadler leads the field through the first turn on lap one of the Allstate 400

Red Bull Formula One driver Christian Klien of Austria passes over the famous red bricks of the Indianapolis Motor Speedway

F-16's fly over Indianapolis Motor Speedway before the start of the 90th running

Indianapolis Motor Speedway, located in Speedway, Indiana is synonymous the motorcar and is older than any other dedicated racing track except the Milwaukee Mile. Speedway was put on the National Register of Historic Places in 1975, and designated a National Historic Landmark in 1987.

The Speedway track is a 2.5 mile (4km) oval cum rectangle that can accommodate over 400,000 spectators and is the largest sporting facility in the world. However, no such splendor was anticipated back on August 19, 1909 when the first race was held here in front of a crowd of 12,000 spectators. The intended distance of 10 miles (16km) was only half complete when the race had to be abandoned. The unstable surface of crushed stone and tar broke up badly injuring a number of drivers and spectators, a few of whom even died. Cars caught fire and the race was canceled with Louis Schwitzer declared the winner.

But thanks to the ambition of former race car driver, automotive parts salesman, and highway pioneer Carl G. Fisher, sufficient money was spent to pave the track with 3.2 million paving bricks. This earned Indianapolis its popular nickname of "The Brickyard."

For $1 admission, an estimated 80,000 spectators came to the Speedway to see the first 500 mile (804.672km) race on Memorial Day (May 30, 1911)— now known as the Indianapolis 500-Mile Race. Ray Harroun won averaging 74.602 mph (120.060 km/h) and "The Greatest Spectacle in Racing" was born. During World War II the track was virtually abandoned for four years and it was feared that racing was lost at the Speedway forever. But Indiana businessman Tony Hulman bought the facility in November 1945 for a reported $750,000. Immediately major renovations and repairs were made in time for the 1946 race. Indy has never looked back.

LAS VEGAS

The Mirage with its spectacular volcano in the foreground

▶ The Las Vegas strip with the colorful turrets of the Excalibur (bottom left) followed by the skyscrapers of New York New York.

▲ The beautiful Bellagio with its majestic water fountainss

▼ The Luxor pyramid crowned with the world's brightest beam of light

Las Vegas in the state of Nevada is famous for its lavish gambling casinos, hotels, and enterainment. It is the center of legalized gambling in the United States. In the 1800s the area that became Las Vegas Valley was still part of Mexico, and was named by Spaniards who used the water here when heading north and west along the Old Spanish Trail from Texas. In May 1855 Nevada was annexed by the United States and Mormon leader Brigham Young quickly sent in 30 missionaries to convert the local Paiute Indians; Mormon influence has remained strong in Las Vegas ever since. In May 1905 Las Vegas was established as a railroad town when land owned by the railroad, was auctioned off and rapidly built on by entrepreneurs, many of them Mormons. Gambling legislation authored by Phil Tobin, a Northern Nevada rancher was designed to raise needed taxes for public schools. Today, more than 43 percent of the state general fund is fed by gambling tax revenue and more than 34 percent of the state's general fund is pumped into public education. By far the most celebrated of the early gambling resorts was the Flamingo Hotel, built by mobster Benjamin "Bugsy" Siegel, a member of the Meyer Lansky crime organization, it opened on New Years Eve 1946, Bugsy was gunned down some 6 months later.

Las Vegas was forced to modernise in 1976, when casino-style gaming was legalized in Atlantic City, New Jersey.

Las Vegas now boasts the most luxurious and biggest Hotel Casino Resorts in the world, with the likes of Caesars Palace, The Mirage, The MGM Grand Hotel & Theme Park, Treasure Island, The Luxor, The Venetian, New York New York, The Mandalay Bay Resort, The Bellagio and The Wynn.

Over 37 million visitors come to Las Vegas each year, one famous visitor stayed so long he was politely asked to leave the Desert Inn, he refused and bought the Casino instead, his name was Howard Hughes.

▲ The forum at the Caesars Palace casino will delight even the most avid shopper

▲ The Mandalay Bay casino resort at the end of the strip boasts a shark-reef aquarium, an 11-acre tropical beach and the Bali Hai Golf Club

MOUNT RUSHMORE

Mount Rushmore in the Black Hills region of South Dakota is named after Charles E. Rushmore, a prominent late 19th century New York lawyer. The Black Hills are sacred to local Native American Indians who fought the U.S. Army nearby at the Battle of Little Bighorn to protect their land. However the location is famous for the huge carved portraits in the rock face of four U.S. presidents.

The motive behind the monument was to attract tourists to the area—it now gets around two million people annually—and finally after long negotiations, on March 3, 1925 Congress authorized the Mount Rushmore National Memorial Commission. The sculptor Gutzon Borglum had already been approached to carve the monument. The original intention was to carve a different set of rocks but they were too eroded and Mount Rushmore was chosen instead. It was at President Coolidge's insistence that two Republicans and one Democrat be portrayed alongside Washington.

The carving to represent the first 150 years of American history started in October 1927 with Borglum and 400 workers making 60ft (18m) sculptures across the rock face and ended in October 1941. The work was done in stages and originally it was intended that each portrait would be carved from head to waist. In 1933 the National Park Service took Mount Rushmore under its jurisdiction. On July 4, 1934, Washington's face was completed and dedicated. Thomas Jefferson was next and dedicated in 1936. The face of Abraham Lincoln was dedicated on September 17, 1937. At this point a bill was introduced in Congress to add the head of civil rights leader Susan B. Anthony but the money was vetoed. In 1939, the face of Theodore Roosevelt was dedicated. When finished the entire project had cost $989,992.32.

PENTAGON

Located in Arlington, Virginia the Pentagon is the headquarters of the United States Department of Defense and is known to those who work there simply as "The Building." The site was decided by President Franklin D. Roosevelt because he didn't want the new building to obstruct the view of Washington, D.C. from Arlington Cemetery as the preferrerd site would have done.

The Pentagon is massive: it is named for its five sides inside which are five floors above ground and five rings of corridors within each floor, plus two basements, making a total of 7.5 miles (28 km) of corridors. Nevertheless it takes no more than seven minutes to walk between any two locations in the building. About 23,000 military and civilian employees work there alongside a further 3,000 non-defense support personnel.,

Building started for the Pentagon on September 11, 1941, and took about sixteen months to complete at a cost to the taxpayer of around $83 million. With steel being at a premium due to the war effort, the building was largely made of concrete processed from 680,000 tons (620,000mt) of sand and gravel dredged from the nearby Potomac River. Dedicated on January 15, 1943 it became the highest-capacity low-rise office building in the world. The open space in the center is known as "ground zero" and is the largest "no-salute, no-cover" area (where U.S. servicemen are exempted from saluting and wearing hats) in the world.

The Pentagon Renovation Program has been ongoing since 1998 and is a major remodeling of the complex requiring complete gutting and reconstruction of the entire building in ordered phases to bring the Pentagon up to modern standards, with greatly improved security. Rebuilding the damaged section of the Pentagon caused by the crash of hijacked American Airlines Flight 77 on September 11, 2001 was named "Phoenix Project."

▲►

The extensive damage caused to the front of the Pentagon, after the September 11th attacks

REDWOOD NATIONAL PARK

The Redwood tree is a living natural wonder being the tallest known plant species in the world as well as one of the longest lived. Their natural habitat lies along the north California coast where to protect them from logging and other dangers Redwood National Park was created in October 1968 along 37 miles of beautiful, untouched California coastline. This was expanded in March 1978 to comprise a total of 112,597.58 acres (45,566ha) of which roughly two thirds are federal and one third belongs to the state. The park is managed in co-operation with three other California State Parks— Prairie Creek Redwoods State Park, Del Norte Coast Redwoods State Park, Jedediah Smith Redwoods State Park—which together protect 45 percent of all the old-growth Coast Redwood forest remaining in California. For 20 million years Redwoods (Sequoia sempervirens) have thrived in this very particular environment—a combination of climate and elevation only found within a few hundred coastal miles. They require the cool moist air blowing in off the Pacific to keep them continually damp, plus over 100in (254cm) of annual rainfall), without this they would rapidly dry out in the sizzling Californian heat. Most Redwoods live on average to around six centuries, and get to a height of around 367ft (122m) with a width of about 22 ft (7m) at the base. Reasons for their longevity include their immunity to disease and resistance to insect damage, principally through their high tannin content and the Redwood's natural ability to withstand forest fires, thanks to their especially thick bark and high foliage canopy. If a Redwood is damaged it has the unusual ability to regenerate itself from a stump or root system and sprout a new tree.

SEARS TOWER CHICAGO

The tallest skyscraper in North America is the Sears Tower in Chicago, Illinois. When it was completed in 1974 it became the tallest building in the world at 1,454ft (443m),and remained so for 22 years until beaten in 1998 by the Petronas Towers in Malaysia.

The Sears Tower was commissioned by the largest retailer in the world, Sears, Roebuck and Company, to consolidate their 350,000 employees who were scattered across the city. Chicago is not called the "Windy City" for nothing, here the average wind speed is 16mph so architect Bruce Graham and structural engineer Fazlur Khan of Skidmore, Owings, & Merrill used a revolutionary bundled-tube structural design of nine steel tubes which gained structural support from a rigid network of beams and columns.

Work started in August 1970 when 114 piles were sunk deep into the earth to stand on solid bedrock, and the first steel was put in place in April 1971. The tower was complete by May 1973 with 108 stories (plus penthouse and roof) and reached 1,451ft (442m) from east entrance to roof top. On a clear day, four states are visible from the top—Illinois, Indiana, Wisconsin, and Michigan. With local service tv antennas added in 1982 and 2000 it reaches 1,729ft (527m). Its 16,100 windows are cleaned by six roof-mounted robotic window-washing machines.

The Sears Tower cost around $150-175 million and was entirely paid for by Sears Roebuck. It was built with space for the company to expand into but would meanwhile rent out. However, the company did not grow as planned and potential lessees did not appear, so the building stood half empty for a decade and by 1995 Sears had sold and moved out altogether. Sears Tower is now a multi-tenant office building containing more than 100 different companies.

STATUE OF LIBERTY

The most iconic symbol of the United States was given in the late 19th century as a gift of friendship and solidarity to commemorate the centennial of the American Declaration of Independence by the Republic of France. Liberty Enlightening the World, better known as the Statue of Liberty, stands proud on Liberty Island (formerly Bedloe's Island) at the mouth of the Hudson River in New York Harbor. French sculptor Frederic Auguste Bartholdi was commissioned in 1876 for the statue which was based on his earlier model that had been intended for Port Said at the entrance of the recently built Suez Canal. The model for Lady Liberty's face might have been his mother or Isabella Eugenie Boyer, the widow of the industrialist Isaac Singer. Bartholdi called in Gustave Eiffel to design the massive iron pylon and secondary skeletal framework.

The people of France were to pay for the statue and its assembly and the Americans for the building of the base. But on both sides of the Atlantic finance proved hard to raise. After much effort sufficient money was raised for the project. In July 1884, 214 crates containing the greater part of the statue (in 350 pieces) was transported to the U.S. on board the French frigate Isere. The right arm and torch already being in New York.

The monument is 305ft (93m) from pedestal to torch, with the statue built from thin copper plates hammered into wooden forms (a process called repoussé), these were then mounted onto a steel skeleton. Lady Liberty wears a crown of seven spikes to represent the seven seas, she holds a torch in her right hand and a tablet saying JULY IV MDCCLXXVI—July 4, 1776, the date of the adoption of the Declaration of Independence in her left.

AMAZON RIVER

The Amazon is a truly mighty river that drains about 40 percent of South America, some 2,722,000 sq miles (6,915,000sq km). It runs all the way through the interior of Peru, right across Brazil and into the Amazon Basin then into the Atlantic at the equator.

Although the Amazon is superseded in size by the River Nile it has by far the greatest total flow of any river, and carries more water than the rivers Mississippi, Nile, and Yangtze combined. In fact the Amazon is credited with contributing a fifth of the total volume of fresh water to the oceans worldwide and the outflow is so strong that it is even noticeable a hundred miles out to sea. Over its lifetime the Amazon has changed its drainage several times: in the early Cenozoic period it drained westwards to the Pacific, but when the Andes uplifted the flow was tilted eastwards to the Atlantic.

The Amazon rises from many springs across the continent but the remotest sources rise from the inter-Andean plateau. The ultimate source was established in 2001 as a stream on a 18,363ft (5,597m) peak called Nevado Mismi in the Peruvian Andes, roughly 99 miles (160km) west of Lake Titicaca. The waters then run generally eastwards for 4,000 miles (6,400km): the Nevado Mismi flows into the Río Apurímac, a tributary of the Ucayali which later joins the Marañón to form the Solimoes, which becomes the Amazon after it meets the Rio Negro near Manaos and moves into the flood plain. For the next 1,000 miles (1,600km) the river lies at its widest and frequently overflows its low banks. In this way the river enters the Amazon rainforest. The Amazon proper is navigable for large ocean steamers up to Manaus, over 900 miles (1,500km) upriver from the mouth.

CHRIST THE REDEEMER

▲

Rio de Janeiro from Corcovado Mountain

High up above Rio de Janeiro in Brazil on top of Corcovado Mountain stands a huge statue of Jesus Christ standing with his arms outstretched blessing the city. Known as O Christo Redentor or Christ the Redeemer, it has become as much a symbol of the city as its famous Copacabana Beach.

The statue on top of the mountain was originally the suggestion of father Pedro Maria Boss back in the 1860. The idea persisted but nothing much happened until the 1920s when fundraising started. Various designs were considered and the competition was intense for the honor. Finally, the design of the Franco-Polish sculptor Paul Landowski was chosen. 1922 marked Brazilian independence and on April 22 that year the foundation stone was placed for the statue. The engineer Heitor de Silva Costa helped with the specifics of the monument and construction finally started in 1927.

The statue was inaugurated in October 12, 1931. It weighs 700 tons (635mt) and stands at the highest point of Corcovado mountain at 2,330ft (710m) on top of a 20ft (6m) pedestal. Christ the Redeemer is 125ft (38m) tall and his open arms measure 98ft (30m) from hand to hand; his left arm points to Rio's zona norte (north zone) and his right towards the zona sul (south zone). It is visible night and day from most parts of Rio.

The same small red train that used to take the workers up the mountain to construct the monument now takes visitors up the mountain every half hour from Cosme Velha. The trip takes 17 minutes and runs almost vertically through the Atlantic Rainforest virtually to the foot of the statue. From there a series of 220 steps runs to the base of the statue, but an escalator has recently been installed.

EASTER ISLAND

▲
A ststue considered to be one of the oldest on the island

▼
Anu Nau Nau

▲
Crater of the volcano Rano Raraku

►
Moai statues at Rano Raraku

Rapa Nui island in the South Pacific is one of the most isolated islands in the world and contains some of the strangest statues ever made. These mysterious Easter Island (as it is called in the west) statues are locally called moai and they are known to have been carved during a relatively short and intense period. However, their exact purpose and meaning is unknown, although many theories have been presented. A total of 887 of these extraordinary statues have been counted although new pieces of statue are occasionally uncovered as ongoing research find more fragments. Archaeologists now estimate that ceremonial site construction and statue carving took place largely between about 1100 A.D. and 1600.

The statues at a first glance appear to be heads, but are in fact the complete torso only with disproportionate sized heads. They tend to stand in lines across the headlands looking out over the sea. Most of the moai were carved out of a distinctive, compressed volcanic ash found at a single site called Rano Raraku. Mysteriously this quarry appears to have been abandoned abruptly, with half-carved statues left still semi-embedded in the rock.

The most widely-accepted theory is that the statues were carved by the ancestors of the Rapanui, Easter Island's modern Polynesian inhabitants, at a time when the island was largely planted with trees and resources were plentiful, enough to support a population of between 10,000-15,000 natives.

The majority of the statues were still standing when the Dutch explorer Jacob Roggeveen (1659-1729) arrived in 1722. Captain James Cook also saw many standing statues when he landed on the island in 1774. But by the mid-19th century, all the statues had been toppled, presumably in internecine wars.

◄
Rapa nui

CHICHEN ITZA

The Maya civilization built the pre-Columbian city complex of Chichen Itza, now a large archaeological site in Yucatán, Mexico. It covers about 3 square miles (4.5km) in area and was mostly built in the late classic period around 800-1000 A.D. It is the most completely restored archaeological site in the Yucatan and attracts visitors from all over the world to the area. The Mayans were a highly cultured but savage people who built an astonishing city full of temples and courts. Much of their religion used blood sacrifice to pacify and please the gods.

Called Chitin Its in Spanish, Itza means "at the mouth of the well of the *Itza* (people)." In the ancient chronicles the city is called Uucyabnal, meaning "Seven Great Rulers." The Yucatán has no above-ground rivers, so the fact that there were three natural sink holes (cenotes) providing plentiful water year round at Chichen made it a natural spot for a center of population.

The city saw its greatest growth and power after the rival Maya sites of the southern central lowlands had collapsed. Although much ruined and covered by jungle the impressive buildings include temples, palaces, stages, markets, baths, and ballcourts. Many of these have now been recovered, the highlights of the site include The Nunnery (Las Monjas), the Church (La Iglesia), the Snail (El Caracol), the Temple of the Warriors, the Temple of Kukulcan (El Castillo)—inside which sits King Kukulcan's Jaguar Throne, carved of stone and painted red with jade spots—an altar-statue known as a Chac Mool, Temple of the Jaguar, and the ball courts which are lined with sculpted panels depicting teams of ball players, with the captain of the winning team decapitating the captain of the losers.

TEOTIHUACAN

Teotihuacán is the largest pre-Columbian city in the Americas, although the name also refers to the civilization this city dominated, which at its peak included much of Mesoamerica. The city is located in the San Juan Teotihuacán in Mexico.

The original name of the city is unknown and it was given the name Teotihuacan by the Aztecs centuries later, a Nahuatl name, which translates as "city where men become gods." According to legend this was where the Gods gathered to plan the creation of man.

The ruined city remained a place of pilgrimage for local peoples but it was "lost" to the outside world until tourists started to visit in the 19th century. Archaeologists started to excavate the site starting in the 19th century but major excavations and renovation began in 1905 on the colossal Pyramid of the Sun for completion by 1910 to celebrate the centennial of Mexican independence. Work on the site has continued since then and is still in progress. The site is so vast that this will continue for decades to come.

At its height Teotihuacan covered over 11 sq miles (30sq km) and contained a population of up to 200,000. The city reached its zenith around 150–450 AD, when it was the center of an influential culture. However the inhabitants of the city do not appear to have developed any written script so remarkably little is known about them, most that is known has been inferred from this site and mentions of the culture from other civilizations.

A huge central avenue runs the length of Teotihuacan, known as the Avenue of the Dead it is flanked by massive ceremonial architecture, including the Pyramid of the Sun, the Pyramid of the Moon, the Temple of Quetzalcoatl, and many lesser temples and palaces.

MACHU PICCHU

Machu Picchu is located high up above the Urubamba Valley in Peru. Because of its isolated position it was forgotten for centuries by the outside world, although not by locals. The invading Spaniards suspected its existence but never found Machu Picchu. It was rediscovered in 1911 by Hiram Bingham, an American historian. Machu Picchu ("Old Peak" in the Quechua language) is a well preserved pre-Columbian Inca ruin romantically located on a high mountain ridge, at an elevation of about 7,710ft (2,350m). The city was probably started in about 1440 by the Sapa Inca Pachacuti and was inhabited until the Spanish conquest of Peru in 1532 and was abandoned some forty years later. Research has shown that Machu Picchu was in effect a country retreat for Inca nobility and possibly a secret ceremonial city.

The site covers about 5 sq miles (13sq km) and is invisible from below and frequently shrouded in clouds. The ruins are cut from the gray granite mountain and comprise palaces, baths, temples, storage rooms, and some 150 houses, all in a remarkable state of preservation. The town was completely self-contained, watered by natural springs, and surrounded by agricultural terraces sufficient to feed the population. An estimated maximum of about 750 people lived in Machu Picchu at any one time, and probably only a small fraction of that number stayed in the town during the rainy season.

One of Machu Picchu's main purposes was that of an astronomical observatory: at midday on March 21st and September 21st, the sun stands almost directly above the Intihuatana ("Hitching Post of the Sun") stone, creating no shadow at all. At this precise moment the sun "sits with all his might upon the pillar" and is for a moment "hitched" to the rock and so is halted in its northward movement.

ANGEL FALLS

The world's highest free-falling waterfall is Salto Ángel or Angel Falls in the Canaima National Park, Venezuela. The water plunges from the Kerepakupay river off Auyantepuy (Devil's Mountain); a tepuy is a flat table-topped mountain with vertical walls. Despite its remote location Angel Falls have become a major tourist attraction. The local Pemon Indians call the falls Churún Merú ("Devil's Mouth").

The waterfall is located in the western part of Canaima National Park which became a protected area on June 12, 1962. The water falls some 3,230ft (979m) with an uninterrupted drop of 2,648ft (807m). Although during the dry season between December and March the water flow is less spectacular.

The falls were first seen by an outsider in the early 20th century by the explorer Ernesto de Santa Cruz, but the falls were not officially "discovered" until 1933 when maverick Missouri aviator James Crawford Angel—who once was a member of Lindbergh's Flying Circus—spotted them while trying to make his fortune while searching for a gold ore bed. Angel returned with companions in 1936 when he landed his plane at the top of the waterfall and set down on the top of Auyan-tepui. However he was unable to fly off again because his Falamingo monoplane had settled down into the marshy ground. Consequently, Angel and his wife, and companions Gustavo Heny, and Heny's gardener, managed to descend the tepui and make their way back to civilization in 11 days. The plane remained there for 33 years before being lifted out by a helicopter and taken to the Aviation Museum in Maracay. Angel told the world about the falls and they came to be called Angel Falls after him. A replica of his monoplane has been placed on top of Auyan-tepui.

AYERS ROCK

The Aboriginal sacred rock Uluru is more commonly known as Ayers Rock and is remotely located in Northern Territory deep in the outback of central Australia, 217 miles (350km) southwest of Alice Springs in Uluru-Kata Tjuta National Park. Uluru is a single massive rock rising straight out of the surrounding plain, it is 5 miles (8km) in circumference and some 986ft (318m) high. But completely hidden, the rock extends for a further 1.5 miles (2.5km) underground. Approximately 500 million years ago Uluru was part of the ocean floor and since being land-bound it has been considerably eroded from its original bulk. The rock contains many springs and waterholes as well as rock caves and aboriginal paintings.

The rock is composed of a coarse-grained sandstone which contains particles of reflective minerals such as feldspar. At sunset and sunrise these crystals reflect the red light giving the already red rock an eerie glow. On the rare occasions when rain falls on Uluru it changes to become a silvery-gray color. In fact the rock is famous for its color changes, depending on the atmospheric conditions and the time of day, it can appear anything from red, black, blue or violet.

The rock was given its western name in 1873 after the then Premier of South Australia, Sir Henry Ayers. Finally after years of controversy, Uluru was returned to the local Pitjantjatjara Aborigines on condition that they would lease it back to the National Parks and Wildlife for 99 years and that it would be jointly managed. The aboriginals do not like strangers climbing their sacred rock and visitors are asked to respect their wishes.

SYDNEY OPERA HOUSE

◄ *The Opera House under construction*   ▲ *The concert hall*

Sydney Opera House is one of the most distinctive and famous 20th century buildings and is gloriously sited on Bennelong Point on the edge of Sydney Harbour, with parkland to its south and Sydney Harbour Bridge nearby.

The opera house was the result of an architectural competition organized in 1957 which asked for a beautiful building, trickily located on a small strip of land jutting out into Sydney Harbour, that could contain two concert halls, which would seat 1,000, and 3,000 people each. The competition drew 233 entries but the winning entry—announced in 1955—was submitted by Jørn Utzon, a largely unknown Danish architect. His distinctive and innovative design looked like a flotilla of sailboats.

Building started in March 1959 and was planned in three stages. The construction of the sail roof proved very problematic and the shapes had to be changed. Unfortunately Utzon felt compelled to leave the project in 1966 following a distinct lack of co-operation from the new Australian government and their refusal to pay his fees. His replacement was Peter Hall.

Money, poor weather, and construction problems dogged the project and by January 1961 it was running 47 weeks late. The controversial design was finally completed in 1973 after 15 years of problems but opened to almost universal acclaim. The final cost was somewhere in the region of $102 million, considerably more than the original estimate of $7 million in 1957.

▲

Mount Tarawera Crater

►

Solitaire Lodge Lake Tarawera peninsula

▲

Whirinaki Forest

▼

Pohutu Geyser

On the southern shore of Lake Rotorua in the Bay of Plenty region of the North Island of New Zealand lies the spa city of Rotorua. The city sits on an ancient volcanic plateau 951ft (290m) above sea level, that covers most of the Central North Island and is still alive with geothermal activity. South and north-east of the city lie the geothermal fields where the crater lakes of the towering volcanoes are constantly refilled with hot, mineral rich waters, making sparkling lakes teeming with wildlife. In ancient times the land was settled by Maori peoples of the Te Arawa iwi and they gave the land the name Te Rotorua-nui-a-Kahumatamomoe (now Rotorua for short). *Roto* means lake and rua means two, thus meaning "second lake," dedicated to Kahumatamomoe. The lake at Rotorua is the largest of many lakes found near the city, and all of which are connected with the Rotorua Caldera and nearby Mount Tarawera.

Geologists can tell from their records that this area has been continually active for millennia. This means everything from hot springs and spouting geysers to bubbling mud pools and drifts of steam and sulfur. In prehistoric times great lava flows swamped the landscape leaving thick layers of mineral deposits. The most recent volcanic eruptions were that of Taupo about 1,800 years ago and the Tarawera eruption on June 10, 1886—only 10 miles (16km) away from Rotorua. Mt Tarawera stands on part of the series of fault lines which form the Pacific "ring of fire." Today there are ten craters along the line of the rift that split the mountain. Although the volcanoes in this area are dormant they still provide enough energy to produce hot geysers—most spectacularly the 66ft (20m) high Pohutu geyser at Whakarewarewa.

◄

Cathedral Rock, Waimangu Volcanic Valley

▲

Wai-O-Tapu Thermal Wonderland